EMOTION REGULATION

Helping Children & Adolescents Take Charge of Their Feelings

Lauren H. Kerstein

Emotion Regulation

Helping Children & Adolescents Take Charge of Their Feelings

All marketing and publishing rights guaranteed to and reserved by:

FUTURE HORIZONS

(817) 277-0727

www.fhautism.com

© 2025 Lauren H. Kerstein

All rights reserved.

No part of this product may be reproduced in any manner whatsoever without written permission of Future Horizons, Inc., except in the case of brief quotations embodied in reviews or unless noted within the book.

ISBN: 978-1-963367-28-7

CONTENTS

WELCOME! V

INTRODUCTION: EMOTION REGULATION VII
    Intended Readership ix
    Emphasis of the Book x
    Goals xii

CHAPTER 1
A STEP TOWARD EMOTION REGULATION: MODELS OF INTERVENTION 1
    Cognitive Behavioral Therapy 1
    Dialectical Behavior Therapy 5
    Positive Psychology 9
    Summary 13

CHAPTER 2
FACTORS, SKILLS, AND TRAITS THAT SUPPORT EMOTION REGULATION 15
    Self-Awareness 15
    Strengths 17
    Specific Skills that Support Effective Emotion Regulation 19
    Traits That Support Emotion Regulation 24
    Summary 26

CHAPTER 3
THE INTERACTION BETWEEN ANXIETY, DEPRESSION, ANGER, AND EMOTION REGULATION 29
    Anxiety 30
    Anxiety in Children and Adolescents 31
    Challenges Associated with Anxiety 36
    Depression 38
    Anger 40
    Next Steps: Examining Specific Intervention Strategies 40
    Summary 43

EMOTION REGULATION

CHAPTER 4
ADDITIONAL INTERVENTION STRATEGIES TO SUPPORT EMOTION REGULATION 45
Learn How to Read Yourself to Be READY 46
Recognize Triggers, Core Beliefs, and Assumptions 50
Evaluate Fight-Flight-Freeze-Fall Asleep Response and Lizard Thinking 66
Assess the Intensity of Emotions 83
Direct Thoughts and Emotions to a Place That Is More Manageable 88
Your Child Is Stronger Than Their Feelings. They Can Be in Charge of Their Feelings and Emotions.. 90
Summary 92

CHAPTER 5
CREATING AN EMOTION REGULATION PLAN FOR THE CHILD: THE REALITY OF EMOTION REGULATION 93
A New Toolbox of Strategies 96

REFERENCES 97

RESOURCES 107

APPENDIX
ASSESSING AND SUPPORTING SKILLS 111
A Brief Note about Assessment Measures 111
A Sample of Areas That Often Require Support 112
EXERCISES AND ACTIVITIES TO SUPPORT EMOTION REGULATION 119

WELCOME!

Working with children and adolescents struggling to manage their emotions is a special privilege that brings with it reward, constant recalibration, and the reality that for all of us, the road to emotion regulation requires tenacity and the proper tools. Thank you for reading this book as part of your journey to help the children or adolescents in your life more effectively manage their emotions.

This book is designed to be used by adults who are assisting children or adolescents in their homes, in schools, or in other settings with identifying strategies that will help them increase their ability to regulate their emotions. The emotion regulation strategies described throughout this book have roots in cognitive behavioral therapy (CBT), dialectical behavior therapy (DBT), and positive psychology. CBT, DBT, and positive psychology are models that show much promise in assisting children who are struggling to regulate their emotions. You will find activities throughout the book that you might want to complete with a child or adolescent. These activities could also be completed independently by the child or adolescent up to the task. Blank versions of these activities are included in the appendix and online.

Special note for caregivers and therapists: Please take a moment to congratulate the child who is reading this with you. If they recognize they need help managing their emotions, they have taken the biggest step in this process: becoming aware. Effective emotion management can lead to more successful relationships, increase the positive feelings the child has about themselves, and help the child's daily life run more smoothly. Managing emotions is a lifelong journey that takes hard work. Remind the child or adolescent that there are times when we all feel more successful than others, and that's okay. The most important part of this journey is to keep moving forward, trying new things, and being kind to ourselves.

EMOTION REGULATION

INTRODUCTION
EMOTION REGULATION

For twenty years I have had the opportunity to spend time with children and adolescents struggling with emotion regulation. Some of these children had received formal diagnoses including but not limited to autism spectrum disorder (ASD), mental health disorders, and attentional disorders. Others had never received nor perhaps warranted a formal diagnosis, but struggled with managing their emotions effectively.

Emotion regulation falls under the complex construct of self-regulation. *Self-regulation* is a person's ability to take control over inner states or responses with regard to thoughts, emotions, attention, and performance (Bell and Deater-Deckard 2007; Vohs and Baumeister 2004). Self-regulation also includes a person's ability to manage the input they receive in their sensory environment.

Emotion regulation has received more intense study in recent years (Igna and Stefan 2015) in light of the fact that the ability to manage emotions underlies many of the skills we need in our everyday lives to be effective socially, sustain friendships, be successful in school, obtain and maintain a job, and find some measure of enjoyment in life (Bell and Deater-Deckard 2007; Denham et al. 2012). Dealing with a pandemic also triggered a lot of much-needed conversations about emotion regulation. Challenges with emotion regulation have also been associated with aggression in childhood (Röll et al. 2012), offering further evidence that it is imperative to study emotion regulation in order to develop effective strategies to mitigate dysregulation.

The regulation of one's emotions can be very difficult. In fact, emotion regulation is a skill as well as a developmental milestone, meaning young children must learn regulation strategies throughout their development. For example, evidence for emotion management has been seen as early as infancy, when at three months of age, infants engage in thumb sucking in order to regulate their arousal levels (Ekas et al. 2013). Thumb sucking is, in essence, an early *coping strategy*—a skill designed to manage emotions more effectively.

In addition, researchers have examined the relationship between emotional awareness, knowledge of emotions, emotion regulation, and school success (Denham et al. 2012). The ability to manage emotions has been found to be predictive of later school success

(Denham et al. 2012). It is, therefore, critical for us to examine emotion regulation and the ways in which to help children and adolescents develop the skills necessary to manage their emotions.

In order to create impactful interventions, it is important to explore early developmental milestones associated with emotion regulation. These include but are not limited to sucking, rooting, head turning, and self-touch (Bridges and Grolnick 1995; Ekas et al. 2013; Kopp 1982). Infants may even learn that playing with or seeking an interesting toy may serve to minimize their distress (Ekas et al. 2013). The development of cognitive and motor skills serves to further increase the infant's use of behavioral strategies to regulate emotions (Ekas et al. 2013). These behavioral strategies include shifting attention away from emotion-eliciting stimuli, shifting attention to the mother, and distracting oneself. All of these behavioral strategies were seen to increase the ability to regulate emotions (Ekas et al. 2013).

Literature examining the development of empathy has also shed light on infants' abilities to understand emotions, react in an empathic manner, and regulate their own emotions (Hutman and DaPretto 2009; Upshaw et al. 2015). These early signs of understanding emotions, reacting empathically, and regulating emotion can include imitating emotions, responding with distress when someone else is distressed (emotional contagion), and matching the emotions of a caregiver (emotion matching) (Hutman and DaPretto 2009).

Research has identified groups of children who may be less likely to develop effective emotion regulation. Individuals with ASD, post-traumatic stress disorder (PTSD), attachment disorder, depression, anxiety, learning challenges, and attention-deficit/hyperactivity disorder (ADHD), as well as other disorders or limitations, often exhibit difficulties with emotion regulation. Due to language barriers, access challenges, and environmental risks, those growing up with socioeconomic disadvantages have been shown to be more at risk for challenges with emotion regulation, as have children from underrepresented populations (Leijten et al. 2015).

Support for emotion regulation is not always included in school intervention plans or deemed worthy of the creation of an educational support plan, despite the fact that many school personnel recognize the relationship between emotion regulation and school success. With or without a formal plan in place, it is critical that teachers and other caregivers know how to use strategies to help children and adolescents regulate their emotions to prevent a possible crisis (e.g., suicide, aggression, interactions with the law) and to increase academic success (Akin-Little et al. 2004; Barnhill and Myles 2001; Fried 2011). Studies in which children received early intervention around emotion regulation have identified a

Introduction

later decrease in internalizing disorders such as anxiety and depression. The studies have also found that the ability to regulate more effectively increased based upon early interventions (Fisak et al. 2011; Rapee 2013). McGilloway et al. (2012) established evidence for positive change for individuals with externalizing disorders (e.g., conduct disorder, ADHD) following support around emotion regulation. It is important, then, to provide early intervention, intervene prior to crises, increase skills, and put supports in place.

This book is a collection of comprehensive, user-friendly strategies rooted in cognitive behavioral therapy (CBT), dialectical behavior therapy (DBT), and positive psychology (PP) that show empirical promise in working with children and adolescents with a variety of diagnosed and undiagnosed challenges.

– A QUICK NOTE ABOUT AUTISM SPECTRUM DISORDERS AND EMOTION REGULATION –

CBT, DBT, and positive psychology have received growing attention as treatment modalities that can effectively support children with ASD (cf. Attwood 2003; Attwood and Garnett 2013; Hartmann et al. 2012; Reaven 2009; White et al. 2009). According to their parents, children with ASD exhibit higher levels of negative affect—anxiety, mood lability, and anger—throughout their lives (White et al. 2009). Emotional state and social functioning are inextricably linked, suggesting the havoc that dysregulated emotional reactions can wreak (Mazefsky et al. 2012). It is, therefore, critical that we find ways to intervene effectively with children with ASD struggling with emotional regulation. In addition to the social risk factors, emotional dysregulation can create tremendous struggles with depression, anxiety, and anger for children on the spectrum.

INTENDED READERSHIP

This book offers specific strategies that can assist children and adolescents with regulating their emotions more effectively. It can be helpful to children who are struggling to manage emotions such as anxiety, depression, or anger but do not necessarily meet the criteria for a specific diagnosis. Many children and adolescents need help with emotion regulation. In fact, at one time or another, all of us need help managing our emotions.

The activities in this book were written to assist clinicians, parents, teachers, and other professionals to think outside the box and support children and adolescents with meaningful, empirically based interventions. Many children and adolescents struggling with mental health difficulties or social interactions exhibit these issues in a way that might be easily misconstrued as willful behavior challenges rather than skill-based deficits. This book looks at emotion regulation as a skill that requires effective interventions.

EMPHASIS OF THE BOOK

As mentioned earlier, this book is designed for adults (teachers, caregivers, clinicians) to use with children and adolescents in order to assist them with developing their ability to regulate their emotions more effectively. Given the importance of teaching self-advocacy and independence, children and adolescents can also be encouraged to try some of the activities independently.

As is true in many situations, prevention is the best intervention. For example, your child is invited to a birthday party to play team sports. Team sports are very stressful for this child due to challenges with gross motor skills, impulsivity, and an intense dislike for situations that involve the potential for losing. You are left with a couple of options:

1. As the caregiver, you can avoid the situation completely and decline the invitation;

2. You can accept but fill your child's toolbox with strategies ahead of time; or

3. You can hope for the best and see what happens.

Depending upon the level of anxiety the birthday party might create for this particular child, you may choose any of these options.

If you choose option A without discussing it with the child, the child won't learn anything. If you choose option A and decide to discuss it with the child, you might explain the fact that there are certain situations that remain challenging for them. You can encourage the child to learn skills that will help them manage their emotions in those situations. This book will help children learn those skills. If you choose option B, this book can help you fill your toolbox with strategies that you can use in a **preventive manner** to assist the child with a more successful birthday party experience. It is also important to discuss this plan with the child to model problem-solving. If you choose option C and the birthday party becomes stressful, you might use the activities in this book to help the child work through challenges **in the moment**. Finally, if you choose options B or C and things do not go as well as you'd hoped (in fact, things go very poorly), you can use the activities to help you

Introduction

process the positives and negatives **after the fact**—once the child (and you) has calmed down and is ready to assess how things went.

This workbook will help adults, children, and teens reach the following goals:

- Develop a better understanding of CBT, DBT, and positive psychology and the ways in which these frameworks can be helpful for somebody struggling with emotion regulation.

- Deepen your understanding of the challenges associated with emotion regulation.

- Create a better understanding of anxiety, depression, and anger and the strategies that CBT, DBT, and positive psychology offer for children wanting to help themselves through their emotional challenges.

- Identify the strengths on which you are building interventions. All interventions must be based upon a solid foundation of strengths in order to be effective.

- Increase strategies for addressing feelings related to anxiety, depression, and anger.

- Identify a link between thoughts, feelings, and actions.

- Increase the ability to be a flexible thinker.

- Identify the "thinking pitfalls" that interfere with progress.

- Create a toolbox of strategies that will consistently and effectively address anxiety, depression, and anger.

- Learn a number of skills that will increase the ability to make and keep relationships.

EMOTION REGULATION

GOALS

If you are reading this book, I assume you have some concerns about a child's emotion regulation. It is often helpful to identify specific goals before trying strategies. Since learning new skills often involves a team effort, teachers, children, and caregivers can work together and align their goals. If you are a teacher, ask yourself, what are your emotion regulation goals for the child? What are the child's goals (to the best of your knowledge) around regulating their emotions? What are the caregivers' goals? Your goals, the child's goals, and the caregivers' goals might be different, and that's okay. It is important, however, that you attempt to find some common ground.

For example, one of your goals may be: My child will identify situations that are challenging for them and pre-plan strategies. Whereas one of the child's goals may be to stay calm at school. These goals are obviously related, and the strategies in this book will offer pathways that help children achieve them. Table 1 (next page) provides sample goals. You will find a blank form in the appendix and online.

Introduction

Table 1: GOALS

Name: _____   Date: _____

Professional	Child/Adolescent	Caregiver
1. My child will identify situations that are challenging for them and pre-plan strategies.	1. I will stay calm at school.	1. My child will understand their emotions better.
2. My child will ask for help when they are struggling to manage their emotions.	2. I will ask my teacher for help when I need it.	2. My child will stay in control of their emotions at school and at home.
3. My child will use strategies (with and without prompting) to help them manage their emotions more effectively throughout the day.	3. I will take a break at school when I need one.	3. My child will use strategies to manage their emotions in difficult situations.

Please note: If writing is a barrier for the child and these activities become arduous as a result, please offer alternatives to writing so the activities can be as meaningful as possible. The activities are designed to provide visual information and feedback based upon research showing that visual supports often make information more meaningful.

CHAPTER 1

A STEP TOWARD EMOTION REGULATION: MODELS OF INTERVENTION

There are a number of **empirically tested** models of intervention that are effective for children and adolescents struggling with emotion regulation. This book will specifically examine and describe intervention strategies that fall under the umbrella of CBT, DBT, and positive psychology.

COGNITIVE BEHAVIORAL THERAPY

CBT is one of the most empirically tested models of treatment in the mental health field across ages and challenges (Bearman and Weisz 2012; Briers 2009; Chahar et al. 2020). The premise of CBT is that thoughts, behaviors, and emotions are connected and that negative thoughts can adversely impact behavior and emotions. Many studies have examined the use of CBT with children and adolescents struggling with developing effective skills for emotion regulation (Chansky 2008, 2014; Szigethy et al. 2012). One such study examined the use of CBT interventions with very young children and found promising results (Hirshfeld-Becker et al. 2008).

Overview

In the 1960s Aaron Beck introduced CBT. This methodology described the impact thoughts and perceptions had on feelings, behaviors, and physiological reactions.

CBT is a hybrid of strategies aimed at eliciting cognitive, behavioral, emotional, and social change (Briers 2009; Szigethy et al. 2012). For the sake of ease in this book, CBT describes therapeutic interventions that address the relationship between thoughts/perceptions, emotions, and behaviors.

EMOTION REGULATION

A Note about Triggers

Much of CBT and DBT focuses on the impact a trigger has on a person's thoughts, feelings, and behaviors. A *trigger* is something that causes an action or reaction. For example, nails on a chalkboard (trigger) cause people to cringe, yell, run out of the room, and generally react negatively. Conversely, the smell of warm vanilla (trigger) might trigger hunger, memories of baking (trigger), excitement over the chance to eat something delicious, and generally positive feelings. Triggers are further explored throughout this book, as they are important to understand. Once children have a better understanding of their triggers, their ability to manage emotional reactions will increase.

Cognitive Behavioral Therapy and Emotion Regulation: Evidence-Based Implications for Practice

Research has been conducted examining the effectiveness of using CBT with children and adolescents struggling with emotion regulation. These studies have shown that CBT is a powerful, effective model for working with children and adolescents struggling with emotion regulation, particularly in the areas of improved coping, decreased emotional dysregulation, and increased emotional awareness (Allen 2011; Hirshfeld-Becker et al. 2008; Rapee 2013; Suveg et al. 2009). The main components of CBT are described below:

1. **Psychoeducation:** Psychoeducation describes the process of helping a child understand that feelings—positive and negative—are universal. Through psychoeducation, children learn to better understand their feelings and identify different skills that will help them more effectively manage their emotions. Psychoeducation also includes education about the fact that emotions like anxiety, for example, are part of the brain's protective response (Chansky 2014).

2. **Somatic management:** Somatic management describes the skills children and adolescents learn to prevent and counter the body's fight-flight-freeze-fall asleep response (Chansky 2014). For example, a child (Dara) might learn to lie on her stomach and spell her name with each breath she takes: **D** (breath) **A** (breath) **R** (breath) **A** (breath)

    This relaxation technique might dissuade her body's fight-flight-freeze-fall asleep response from activating or calm that response before it increases.

Chapter 1

3. **Cognitive restructuring:** Cognitive restructuring describes the process by which a child or adolescent recognizes negative automatic thinking and learns to flip those thoughts to more realistic, adaptive thoughts that will help facilitate effective emotion regulation (Chansky 2014).

4. **Problem-solving:** Problem-solving involves developing strategies that assist the child or adolescent in emotionally charged situations. It is helpful to identify specific situations in which the problem strategies might be most useful.

5. **Exposure:** Exposure includes gradual, systematic, and controlled experiences with feared situations in order to realize the fears about the situation are not realistic (Chansky 2014; Velting et al. 2004).

6. **Relapse prevention:** Relapse prevention includes devising a plan that will assist a child with avoiding setbacks and generalizing strategies across multiple environments and situations.

Let us look at how CBT might be helpful for Jonathan. Jonathan is a third grader who demonstrates characteristics of ASD but has never received a formal diagnosis. He struggles with sustaining friendships, emotion regulation, and anxiety and is sensitive to auditory stimuli. The following situation often arises, disrupting Jonathan's friendships. Jonathan is quick to make a new friend and then spends a lot of time with that one friend. Inevitably, the friend does something that triggers Jonathan's auditory sensitivities, such as loud chewing, humming, singing, or some other loud noise, and Jonathan perceives this stimulus as purposeful and hurtful. These moments usually end with Jonathan screaming at the friend, thereby effectively ending the friendship and leaving Jonathan with more anxiety and chronic stomachaches until he finds a new friend.

1. **Psychoeducation:** In Jonathan's case, psychoeducation around his auditory sensitivity, distorted thinking, and subsequent anxiety could help him shift his perspective in social interactions. A shift in perspective might help Jonathan move from feeling attacked to recognizing that the peer's actions were just mundane, non-purposeful activities that triggered an emotional reaction in him. If he were able to look at the interaction through the lens of *accidental irritation* versus *purposeful irritation*

on the part of his friend, he might react differently, be in control of his emotional response, and maintain the friendship.

2. **Somatic management:** Jonathan's fight-flight-freeze-fall asleep response seems to be triggered when he hears a loud or noxious sound. Pairing psychoeducation regarding triggers and distorted thinking with strategies that can calm his body in a challenging situation might assist Jonathan with emotion regulation.

3. **Cognitive restructuring:** Jonathan's automatic thinking that his friend was intentionally trying to upset him caused an emotional meltdown. If Jonathan were able to examine the evidence available (Chansky 2014) in the situation, he would be able to flip his thoughts to ones that supported emotion regulation rather than aggravated the process. A more realistic coping thought for Jonathan might be: "My friend is making a loud noise, and he doesn't realize it's bothering me."

4. **Problem-solving:** Once Jonathan can normalize his anxiety and recognize the situations that are most triggering for him, he can develop strategies that will best assist him through the stressful situations.

5. **Exposure:** Exposure to different noises and learning ways to cope with the noises more effectively would be helpful for Jonathan. These new coping strategies would then assist him when triggering situations arise with a friend.

6. **Relapse prevention:** Creating a toolbox of strategies for Jonathan; clearly identifying the situations, people, and triggers that are challenging; and developing clear (visual) supports that Jonathan can use will help him avoid setbacks in his ability to manage emotions.

Specific intervention strategies for emotion regulation incorporating CBT are described in chapters 3, 4, and 5.

Chapter 1

– A QUICK NOTE ABOUT AUTISM SPECTRUM DISORDER –

The components of CBT (as described above), including psychoeducation, somatic management, cognitive restructuring, problem-solving, exposure, and relapse prevention (Velting et al. 2004) have been embedded in a number of treatment programs aimed at children struggling with emotion regulation, including but not limited to children and adolescents on the spectrum (Chalfont et al. 2007; Reaven et al. 2009, 2012; Sofronoff et al. 2007; Wood et al. 2009). These treatment programs include but are not limited to the following: Facing Your Fears: Group Therapy for Managing Anxiety for Children with High-Functioning ASD (Reaven et al. 2012); The Coping Cat program (Keehn et al. 2013); and Multi-Component Integrated Treatment (White et al. 2010).

DIALECTICAL BEHAVIOR THERAPY

DBT is an empirically tested model of treatment that falls under the umbrella of CBT and combines individual therapy with work on specific skills, including mindfulness, interpersonal effectiveness, emotion regulation, and distress tolerance (Hartmann et al. 2012). DBT is emerging as a treatment that has promise for working with children and adolescents struggling with emotion regulation challenges (Harvey and Penzo 2009; MacPherson et al. 2013).

Overview

DBT aims to assist children with emotion dysregulation symptoms and related behavioral challenges as seen across mental health disorders (Kring and Sloan 2010). Based on CBT, DBT has been shown to be effective in developing skills to manage distress and intense emotions without becoming out of control or acting destructively (McKay et al. 2007; Valentine et al. 2015).

DBT has roots in many of the theories that ultimately shaped CBT. These theories include classical behaviorism, reinforcement (negative or positive), extinction, and shaping (Hadjiosif 2013). DBT examines the ways in which identifying triggers can lead to the development of effective coping strategies. The ability to recognize triggers and develop effective coping strategies supports increased well-being. Finally, DBT embraces the importance of a close therapeutic relationship in effecting change (Bass et al. 2014; Feigenbaum 2007).

DBT was designed to assist adolescents and adults with (a) developing new skills, (b) consistently using these skills, and (c) learning to generalize these skills across multiple contexts (Feigenbaum 2007). Linehan (1993) looked at mindfulness as a critical component in developing self-regulation. Mindfulness, rooted in Eastern philosophy and dialectics, describes the ability to observe, describe, and be in the universe without judging or experiencing self-consciousness (Hartmann et al. 2012). For example, one of the key components of DBT is *radical acceptance*, which means accepting or embracing a situation even if we do not like it. Radical acceptance also includes the knowledge that there are some things we can't control in others and ourselves but that we can do our best despite difficult situations.

DBT incorporates individual therapy and group skills training sessions that help children and adolescents self-soothe, regulate emotional reactions, manage stress, validate dysfunctional cognitions as real, and achieve radical acceptance (meaning acceptance of all thoughts, ideas, and experiences without judgment) (Jennings and Apsche 2014). These processes help clients develop critical skills, control negative self-judgments (which perpetuate challenges), and develop skills to manage distressing, intense emotions.

Dialectical Behavior Therapy and Emotion Regulation: Evidence-Based Implications for Practice

DBT has been adapted for use with children, adolescents, and adults with varying diagnostic challenges in order to work on emotion regulation and distress tolerance, including college students with self-injurious behavior (Engle et al. 2013); adolescents with various psychiatric disorders (Groves et al. 2012; MacPherson et al. 2013); eating disorders (Lenz et al. 2013); ADHD (Feigenbaum 2007; Hesslinger et al. 2002; Perepletchikova et al. 2011); ASD (Hartmann et al. 2012); and other mental health challenges (Valentine et al. 2015).

DBT teaches four skills through skills training that are critical to managing life's stressors and accompanying emotions:

1. **Distress tolerance:** Distress tolerance describes a person's ability to cope with difficult events.

2. **Mindfulness:** Mindfulness is the ability to remain in the present rather than focusing on the past or future.

3. **Emotion regulation:** Emotional regulation is the ability to examine and modulate feelings.

Chapter 1

4. **Interpersonal effectiveness:** Interpersonal effectiveness refers to the ability to interact effectively with others, get one's needs met, and protect the relationship (McKay et al. 2007).

Let's look at ways in which interventions designed to address distress tolerance, mindfulness, emotion regulation, and interpersonal effectiveness may be helpful for children and adolescents like Greg, who struggles with generalized anxiety disorder.

Greg is a fifteen-year-old freshman at a large high school. Greg received a diagnosis of generalized anxiety disorder at nine years old. On the first day of school (three months ago), Greg was bullied as he walked to English class. The administration supported Greg and intervened. Greg also received assistance from the school social worker to work through the trauma the situation created. However, since then, Greg's heart races and palms sweat every time he walks to English class. He has never encountered the bully again (the bully switched schools shortly after the incident). One day, Greg was walking down the hallway past the spot where he was bullied and a child Greg had never seen before approached him. As soon as Greg saw the child approach, he looked down and quickened his pace. The child said something to him, but Greg did not hear what he said. He assumed the boy was going to bully him just like the first boy. He thought his walk to English class must be cursed. He thought there was something wrong with him because these incidents kept happening, and he became increasingly angry with himself for reacting with fear once again. Greg continued walking, lost in his swirling thoughts. His pulse quickened as he remembered the initial bullying event. Finally, the peer caught up with him and said, "Hi, I'm Jake. Wow, you sure walk fast. You dropped your papers, and I thought you'd want them."

1. **Distress tolerance:** The validation and "radical acceptance" components of distress tolerance could be helpful to Greg because they offer acknowledgment and validation for challenges while simultaneously helping him move toward accepting lingering discomfort and difficulties. Feelings of validation and acceptance could potentially lead Greg to shine a spotlight or turn up the volume on his strengths rather than his struggles. In addition, acceptance of the facts of a situation can also assist with tolerating and managing a difficult situation (Swales 2009). If a caring adult could have helped Greg better understand his fear reaction and recognize that Jake triggered him to remember an incident that was scary (but that happened in the past), he might have been able to manage his reaction more effectively. Greg's situation suggests he suffered from post-traumatic stress disorder (PTSD) following

the previous incident. A discussion about PTSD exceeds the scope of this book. It is important to note, however, that PTSD significantly influences emotion regulation. A critical component in working with children struggling with PTSD is helping them recognize the current events that trigger past negative memories. Recognizing triggers will help children begin to identify helpful interventions.

2. **Mindfulness:** Learning mindfulness, the ability to be present in one's environment (and not in one's head or thoughts), might enhance Greg's ability to examine his surroundings, including the nonverbal and contextual clues that would lead to a better understanding of the social world. There are several ways to teach mindfulness, some of which will be described later in this book. If Greg had been more mindful in this situation, he might have noticed Jake holding his papers out to him as he walked. This level of mindfulness might have changed the entire experience and interaction.

3. **Emotion regulation:** The skills training would support the development of skills to regulate emotions more effectively. If Greg had emotion regulation skills, his reaction to the situation with Jake would have looked very different. He might have been able to manage his feelings and interrupt his immediate retrieval of a past memory so he could interact with Jake rather than "run" from him. In addition, the **dialectical component** of DBT, and the concepts that (a) everything is part of a whole system, (b) change is inevitable, and (c) there are opposing views in each situation, could encourage Greg to increase his ability to be cognitively flexible. Cognitive flexibility leads to more effective emotion regulation. Greg focused on one contextual detail—the fact that he was walking to English and a boy approached him just like the day he was bullied, but he was unable to look at the other contextual clues and variables to formulate a more accurate big-picture understanding of the situation. As a result of these challenges, he was unable to regulate his emotions.

4. **Interpersonal effectiveness:** DBT's focus on effective interpersonal interactions could be helpful. We can teach Greg to approach others in a gentle way that includes a readiness to listen and flexible thinking. We can also assist Greg with learning to be assertive in an effective versus aggressive way. Role-plays are a useful way to teach these skills. Greg's fear reaction and inability to modulate his emotional reaction greatly interfered with his ability to respond to Jake effectively. Using role-plays

to practice interpersonal effectiveness might greatly help Greg in future interactions. Specific interventions to assist with the development of relationship skills are briefly discussed in the appendix. In addition, one of the goals of DBT is to assist with **generalization** (Feigenbaum 2007). Although Greg received assistance with managing his emotions following the bullying incident, he did not learn how to generalize those emotion-management skills to other situations. Generalization of skills is a critical tool to learn in order to manage emotions effectively across multiple environments.

– A QUICK NOTE ABOUT AUTISM SPECTRUM DISORDER –

Given the tendency for children with ASD to encounter significant struggles with emotion regulation (Hartmann et al. 2012), the components of DBT (as described above), including distress tolerance, mindfulness, emotion regulation, and interpersonal effectiveness (McKay et al. 2007) have been explored as helpful interventions to incorporate into work with children with ASD (Hartmann et al. 2012). While the research is still evolving and modifications are still being explored (Hartmann et al. 2012), DBT is a promising treatment modality for children and adolescents with ASD (Mazefsky and White 2014).

POSITIVE PSYCHOLOGY

Positive psychology is a relatively new model in the mental health field that is proving helpful based on research (Peterson 2006). *Positive psychology* is the scientific study of the components of life that go right. Traditionally, the mental health field studied human problems and remedies rather than what goes right with people. As such, positive psychology challenges the disease model and encourages people to focus on strengths (Peterson 2006). While the literature regarding positive psychology and children is limited, it seems an important model to examine with regard to supporting children struggling with emotion regulation. Positive psychology's focus on the science of well-being, hope, self-efficacy, optimism, courage, gratitude, and positive development could be quite beneficial to children struggling with effectively regulating their emotions (cf. Linehan, 1993; Marques et al. 2011; O'Grady 2013).

EMOTION REGULATION

Overview

Positive psychology suggests that the aspects of a person's life that are good are as important and require equal attention to the aspects of a person's life that are difficult (Peterson 2013). In particular, building resilience is the guiding principle behind positive psychology. CBT and DBT also support children's ability to build their resilience in the face of emotional stressors.

Martin Seligman popularized the use of the phrase *positive psychology* (Seligman 1991). Positive psychology is derived from a rich and diverse history and theories, including resilience, psychological well-being, factors that contribute to health, and protective factors (attributes of a person or environmental conditions) that help a person weather life's storm rather than being washed away in a puddle of despair and distress.

Positive Psychology and Emotion Regulation: Evidence-Based Implications for Practice

The research on positive psychology for emotion regulation challenges in children and adolescents has shown promising results both in classroom-wide intervention strategies and intervention programs geared toward individual children and adolescents (Groden et al. 2011; Marques et al. 2011; Owens and Patterson 2013; Seligman et al. 2009).

Students with anxiety, depression, ASD, ADHD, and other developmental or mental health challenges have unique strengths that often end up brushed aside in our pathology-based world. Peterson (2006) believed individuals have "signature strengths" (p. 158) and that the ability to capitalize and use these signature strengths can be quite fulfilling.

The University of Pennsylvania hosts a website called Authentic Happiness that has a ten-minute survey to explore areas of strength (https://www.authentichappiness.sas.upenn.edu/testcenter). It might be helpful to explore this survey to help children and adolescents learn their signature strengths. The key, however, is to encourage children to be as honest with themselves as possible and to err on the side of viewing themselves in a positive light rather than a negative one. An understanding of strengths will support children and adolescents on the journey to managing their emotions. Note that you'll need to register on the site to take their surveys.

There are three pillars of positive psychology:

1. **Positive subjective experience:** Positive subjective experience can include happiness, pleasure, joy, gratification, and fulfillment.

Chapter 1

2. **Positive individual traits:** Positive individual traits can include strengths of character, talents, interests, values, hope, optimism, kindness, humor, self-efficacy, and resilience (Peterson 2007; Groden et al. 2011).

3. **Positive institutions:** Positive institutions include families, schools, businesses, communities, and societies.

Let us look at the ways positive psychology might be helpful for Natasha:

Natasha is a sixth grader who has never received a formal assessment or diagnosis. She is a very strong student who typically excels in math and reading. She is quite hard on herself about her grades and often spends hours studying for tests and completing homework. In the past couple of weeks, her grades have declined. About a month ago, Natasha had a surprise quiz and did very poorly. Ever since then, she has refused to try new things academically. The more her grades fall, the more depressed and hopeless she becomes.

1. **Positive subjective experience:** The first step in supporting Natasha may be to increase the experiences she has in her life that increase happiness, pleasure, joy, gratification, and fulfillment. As she struggles in class, she seems to be losing sight of the aspects of her life that are going well. It might be helpful to note these aspects in a visual way so Natasha can conceptualize the positives. In addition, it is important to add experiences back into Natasha's life that will bring her joy, thus bolstering her in this difficult time.

2. **Positive individual traits:** It seems Natasha has lost sight of the positive traits she has that might help her find her way through this challenging situation. Let's focus for a moment on resilience, in particular. As mentioned above, resilience is the ability to bounce back after stressful situations. People who are resilient are able to manage stressors and associated emotional storms and come out functioning well (Henderson 2012). Students who are resilient generally have hope, can engage in flexible thinking, have good interpersonal skills, and are able to view the world through a more optimistic lens (Henderson 2012). Natasha struggled to bounce back from a poor grade on a test and, in fact, developed anxiety around her ability to perform. This anxiety paralyzed her. Using the positive psychology framework, we can assist children like Natasha in becoming more resilient by (a) teaching them

the skills they need to be flexible thinkers, (b) working to increase their interpersonal skills, and (c) teaching them strategies to manage emotions.

3. **Positive institutions:** Finally, as we assist children like Natasha, we want to mobilize the external support (places and people) that can be helpful. Natasha may need a tutor who can help her out of the academic slump she has entered. The teacher may need to offer extra credit projects and other assignments that could boost Natasha's competence and confidence. Finally, outside support can continue to help Natasha see her strengths as more salient than her challenges.

As you begin interventions with the child or adolescent, select one strength on which to build. For example, humor can increase resilience. Perhaps you are working with a child who appreciates humor, is an excellent joke teller, or has a wonderful sense of sarcastic humor. We as clinicians, parents, professionals, and caregivers can help the children and adolescents in our care capitalize on a strength like humor in their journey toward emotional regulation.

– A QUICK NOTE ABOUT AUTISM SPECTRUM DISORDER –

The components of positive psychology, including positive subjective experiences, positive individual traits, and positive institutions, have been explored and incorporated into treatment for individuals with ASD. In their book, Groden et al. (2011) examine how positive psychology can assist individuals on the autism spectrum. They focus specifically on resilience, optimism, humor, kindness, and self-efficacy. In addition, Zager (2013) explores the ways in which positive psychology can increase quality of life and emotional well-being and regulation for children with ASD as they learn to focus on strengths and positive thinking. Focusing on strengths and moving away from negativity can increase proactive behavior and adaptive reactions to life's situations.

Chapter 1

SUMMARY

The remainder of this book focuses on interventions that are based on either CBT, DBT, positive psychology, or a combination thereof in order to illustrate specific, concrete strategies that might assist children in increasing emotion regulation. The intervention section of the book begins with an examination of factors, skills, and traits associated with emotion regulation and interventions that increase these skills. The more we increase children's skills, the better they will do in their environments. We will then move to emotion regulation strategies that are rooted in CBT, DBT, and positive psychology.

CHAPTER 2
FACTORS, SKILLS, AND TRAITS THAT SUPPORT EMOTION REGULATION

It is important to consider the factors, skills, and traits that contribute to and facilitate effective emotion regulation. Working toward a goal is like climbing a ladder. Each rung of the ladder is a building block toward the ultimate goal.

In this chapter, we will take a look at each rung on the emotion regulation ladder. First, we will examine self-awareness and strengths. Each of these factors is an important rung on the self-regulation ladder.

Next, we will examine the specific skills that facilitate more effective emotion regulation, paying particular attention to interoception, motor skills, theory of mind, flexible thinking, and communication and pragmatic language skills. While a thorough assessment of each of these skills is outside the scope of this book, the following discussion is meant to increase your awareness and help you visualize intermediate goals or rungs that might require strengthening in order to reach the ultimate goal of emotion regulation.

Finally, we will highlight the traits that support effective emotion regulation, including temperament, resilience, and emotional intelligence. These traits propel a person up the proverbial ladder in order to reach their goal of emotion regulation.

As mentioned, a thorough evaluation or assessment is outside the scope of this book. The appendix offers a few assessment tools and intervention strategies that will help children and adolescents strengthen areas that you agree are particularly challenging.

SELF-AWARENESS

The first step in assisting a child develop emotion regulation skills is to help them increase self-awareness, specifically around emotion regulation. Self-awareness is the key to motivation, investment, and progress. If the child doesn't recognize their challenges and strengths, they will not necessarily understand the purpose of developing new skills.

One way to increase self-awareness is through self-assessment. Help the child or adolescent you are working with answer the following questions in table 2.1 using a 1–5 scale

EMOTION REGULATION

where 1 means *strongly disagree*; 3 means *neutral* about the statement; and 5 means *strongly agree*. Numbers 2 and 4 mean the child leans more toward agreeing or disagreeing. Discuss the number that best represents how the child feels (Gross and John 2003). Table 2.1 can also be found in the appendix and online.

Table 2.1: MY EMOTION REGULATION

Name: _____   Date: _____

Directions: Answer the following questions using a 4-point scale.
1 = strongly disagree;   2 = agree;   3 = disagree;   4 = strongly disagree.

1. When I want to feel more *positive* emotions (such as joy or amusement), I change what I'm thinking about.	1	2	3	4
2. I keep my emotions to myself.	1	2	3	4
3. When I want to feel fewer *negative* emotions (such as sadness or anger), I change what I'm thinking about.	1	2	3	4
4. I am a person who takes control of my emotions by managing my thoughts and reactions.	1	2	3	4
5. I let my feelings drive my thoughts and reactions.	1	2	3	4

If the child or adolescent requires support to answer questions 4 and 5, you can use the following example to help you as you explore this with them:

"Imagine you just found out that you are not going to be able to buy Brand A boots because they are too expensive. You only want Brand A boots. Will you stop to regroup before talking about it, or will you act impulsively and let emotions rule your actions?"

You can also ask the child whether they can express emotions in a helpful way. Do they find that they stuff their emotions in or let them out slowly and thoughtfully? You can use the following example in your conversation:

Chapter 2

"The last two weeks at school have been very stressful. You didn't do as well on a test as you wanted to, your good friend seems angry with you, and you are worried about your brother, who has to have surgery. Ask them if they will use strategies that help them slowly let the "air" out of their feeling balloon so that it will not become too full and "pop," or stuff their feelings because they do not want to deal with them. Remind the child or adolescent that stuffing causes the balloon to expand until it becomes increasingly likely that it will explode."

Figure 2.1

These kinds of conversations will help children better understand their ability to regulate emotions and increase their desire to strengthen their skills. Remember, increasing the child's understanding of their ability (or inability) to regulate is a very important intervention tactic because it will help them better identify times they need to implement strategies that increase effective emotion regulation.

STRENGTHS

Emotion regulation is a skill. If regulating emotions is challenging for a child or adolescent in your care, please remember that emotion regulation skills can be **learned**. The interventions in this book will help children take a step toward more effective emotion regulation. For all of us, in our attempt to learn skills, interventions are always more effective when our strengths are incorporated. When asked to do things outside of our natural skills, it is much harder to accomplish the task and feel any sense of competence. For example, accounting is *not* an area of strength for me. Therefore, tax season (and the tasks associated with doing my taxes) is stressful for me. On the other hand, organization and recordkeeping is a strength for me. During tax season, I rely on my organizational and recordkeeping skills and look for outside assistance with accounting. My strength-based approach ensures my taxes will be filed correctly.

My guess is that the children in your care have strengths and challenges as well. Examples of strengths are listed in table 2.2.

You may encourage the child to check off the strengths that resonate with them.

EMOTION REGULATION

Table 2.2: STRENGTHS

Name: _____   Date: _____

__ The ability to notice small details and pieces of information

__ The ability to look at the big picture in a situation

__ The ability to think deeply about a topic

__ The ability to be organized

__ The capacity for empathy

__ The ability to be kind

__ A talent in logical reasoning

__ An interest in morality and rules

__ The ability to memorize information quickly

__ A large vocabulary

__ A lot of knowledge about particular subjects

__ An inquisitive nature

__ A good memory

__ A sense of humor

__ The ability to pick up on new information quickly

__ The ability to form close relationships

__ The desire to help others

__ The desire to please others

__ Other (please complete)

__ Other (please complete)

Now, take a moment to think about the strengths of the children or adolescents with whom you spend time. I challenge you to turn to the appendix and write down five strengths for one child in ten seconds in table 2.3. Then challenge the child to do the same. A sample is below.

Ready ... Set ... Go!

Table 2.3: STUDENT STRENGTHS

Name: _____   Date: _____

The child or adolescent has the following strengths:

1. Kind
2. The desire to please others
3. A sense of humor
4. The ability to notice small details
5. Empathy

This child or adolescent is also good at:

6. Visual decoding
7. Art
8. Recognizing patterns
9. Compassion
10. Persistence

Chapter 2

After you and the child complete your respective forms, discuss the results of both. Share your thoughts about their strengths. Ask the child about the strengths they have observed in themselves. Observing, noting, and building upon strengths increases the likelihood that interventions will be effective. (And boosts confidence along the way.)

As discussed in Appendix 1, the Underlying Characteristics Checklist (UCC) and the Individual Strengths and Skills Inventory (ISSI) (Aspy and Grossman 2011) may provide helpful frameworks through which to evaluate children's strengths and challenges.

– A QUICK NOTE ABOUT AUTISM SPECTRUM DISORDER –

Children on the autism spectrum are quite heterogeneous. In the words of Dr. Stephen Shore, "If you've met one person with autism, you've met one person with autism." It is critical, then, for children and adolescents with autism, and for that matter, all children, no matter their diagnosis (or lack thereof), to assess their specific areas of strengths and challenges in order to design the most meaningful and effective interventions.

SPECIFIC SKILLS THAT SUPPORT EFFECTIVE EMOTION REGULATION

In my clinical experience and in reviewing the emotion regulation literature, there are a number of skills associated with the development of emotion regulation. As you review the skills below, imagine they are rungs on the emotion regulation ladder or gears that keep the emotion regulation machine running. Figure 2.2: The Emotion Regulation Machine illustrates this relationship.

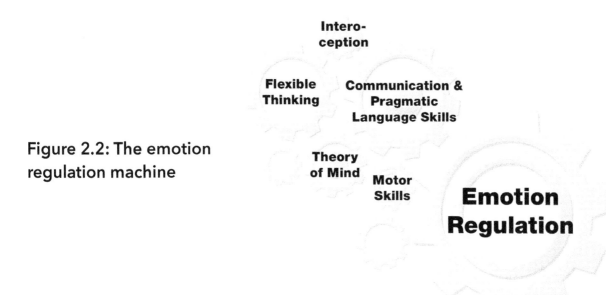

Figure 2.2: The emotion regulation machine

EMOTION REGULATION

It is important to note that although some of these skills seem unrelated to emotion regulation, any challenge that has the potential to increase anxiety, anger, sadness, or frustration impacts emotion regulation. Let's turn to Bob.

Bob has trouble reading social cues. As a result, social situations, and especially recess, cause him a great deal of anxiety. One day, Bob's anxiety was particularly high. When a peer threw a ball to Bob in an effort to begin a game of catch, the ball hit Bob in the face. Bob misunderstood and thought the peer was intentionally hitting him with the ball and punched the peer. Bob's increased anxiety and anger interfered with not only his ability to regulate his emotions, but also his ability to make a thoughtful decision. Intensity of emotions directly impacts decision making.

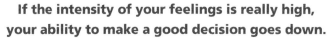

Figure 2.3: Emotion intensity and decision making from *My Sensory Book* by Lauren H. Kerstein, LCSW

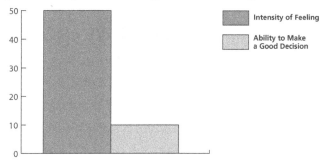

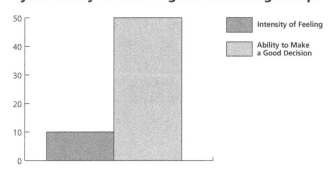

Chapter 2

Therefore, we must work to increase our skills in order to keep the intensity of our emotions at a more manageable level. As you review the following skills, think about whether or not they are a strength or a weakness for the children with whom you work. If you determine they are an area of weakness, the Appendix: Assessing and Supporting Skills, offers interventions that will help children strengthen these skills. The stronger each of these skills are, the better the child or adolescent will be able to regulate their emotions.

Interoception

Interoception, which has been called the "eighth sensory system" (Mahler 2015), refers to the ability to perceive the internal state of one's body. Feelings come from inside our body. A tight neck or fluttery stomach are often signs of a particular feeling. Interoception helps us identify how our body feels so we can recognize our emotional reactions, and identify feelings. Interoception helps us understand how we feel (Craig 2002). Interoception is associated with both emotion regulation and empathy. Children who have challenges with interoceptive awareness (IA) and are unable to identify the state of their body or their emotional experience will then have trouble regulating their emotions. In her work, Mahler (2015) focuses specifically on challenges that people with autism spectrum disorders have with interoception. Given the fact that IA is a key player in not only recognizing emotion but regulating it, it is important to strengthen this skill in the child or adolescent. A brief overview of strategies for increasing IA may be found in the Appendix. You might also want to refer to Mahler's book *Interoception: The Eighth Sensory System: Practical Solutions for Improving Self-Regulation, Self-Awareness and Social Understanding of Individuals with Autism Spectrum and Related Disorders* for more information.

Motor Skills

Although it may seem counterintuitive that motor skills can impact emotion regulation, they do, in fact, play a role in emotion management. This role is twofold. First, challenges with motor skills can cause anxiety, anger, or frustration, which, in turn, can lead to dysregulation. Second, motor skills contribute to our ability to meet emotional needs. For example, as mentioned earlier, the infant development literature noted that infants might reach for an interesting toy in order to distract themselves from an emotion-loaded situation (Ekas et al. 2013). If the infant did not have the motor coordination to obtain the interesting toy and was subsequently unable to distract themselves, this might lead to emotional dysregulation. Similarly, if a child did not have the motor coordination to write quickly or fluidly, this would impact their ability to complete schoolwork and increase negative feelings.

Difficulties with motor skills can include the following:

1. **Motor planning**—the ability to sequence steps for both novel and familiar tasks (Ayres 2005). Motor planning requires the brain to communicate with the body so you can visualize the task and sequence the steps necessary to complete the tasks. Motor planning is required for such tasks as dressing, playing a sport, riding a bicycle, and tying your shoes.

2. **Fine motor**—delays in the ability to complete small-motor movements, such as opening a jar, writing, drawing, eating, and buttoning clothes.

3. **Gross motor**—delays with large-motor movements, such as those required for walking, running, hopping, jumping, skipping, and catching a ball.

Theory of Mind

Theory of mind (ToM) describes a person's ability to recognize and understand others' mental states, thoughts, feelings, perspectives, motivations, and beliefs (Flavell 1999). ToM also examines a person's ability to recognize their own emotions and perspectives (Schipper and Petermann 2013).

One of the theories regarding relationship skill challenges points to difficulties with theory of mind (Cotugno 2009; Yeh 2013). If a person has trouble understanding others' mental states, perspectives, motivations, thoughts, feelings, and beliefs, it is difficult to interact effectively, which can cause dysregulation. ToM and its interaction with relationship skills is a critical component of emotion regulation. Relationship skills include but are not limited to "reading" nonverbal information (body posture and cues), referencing, eye contact, attending, regulating, coordinating social interactions, reciprocity (the back-and-forth in social interactions), social perception, and a general desire to seek shared enjoyment with another person.

Understanding and accurately recognizing emotions is the heart of ToM. If a person experiences challenges labeling, recognizing, and understanding their own emotional states, this can lead to emotion regulation difficulties (Schipper and Petermann 2013). Understanding emotions in oneself and in others is the core of learning effective emotion regulation.

Studies have examined the relationship between ToM and empathy (Decety and Jackson 2006; Mathersul et al. 2013) given the fact that empathy comes from an understanding of the ways in which a person may experience an event. Empathy is linked to the ability to regulate emotions more effectively (Schipper and Petermann 2013).

Flexible Thinking

Another pitfall to emotion regulation is rigid thinking. It is critical, therefore, that we teach our children how to be flexible thinkers. Flexible thinking is one of the domains of a larger concept called *executive function* (Dawson and Guare 2004; 2009).

Thinking in a flexible way, or rainbow thinking, can be challenging. The challenge with rainbow thinking is that people often believe that rigidity leads to greater control over situations and a subsequent decrease in negative feelings (Kerstein 2013). The opposite, however, is true. The more inflexible a person becomes, the less control they have, and the greater the opportunity for anxiety, depression, and anger. In their book *How to be Brainwise: The Proven Method for Making Smart Choices*, Patricia Gorman Barry talks about the problem-solving benefits of using your wizard brain (flexible-thinking brain) versus your lizard brain (primitive, reptilian brain). When we are able to use our wizard over our lizard brain, our feelings generally become more positive, and our choices more helpful.

Figure 2.4: Our thinking impacts our feelings.

Incorporating tools to increase flexible thinking may help the child increase their ability to regulate their emotions. The appendix offers a number of strategies to consider.

EMOTION REGULATION

Communication and Pragmatic Language Skills

Challenges with communication and pragmatic language skills are often associated with ASD. Many other children and adolescents, however, may struggle with delays in speech-language development, recognizing and decoding nonverbal communication, literal interpretations of language, repetitive or stereotyped language, reciprocity, comprehension, literacy, auditory processing, articulation, speech rhythm, tone, and pitch.

Pragmatic language skills are the social components of language. They include idioms, figures of speech, expressions, and the common lingo of the time. Pragmatics also includes knowing what to say, how to say it, and when to say it (Bowen 2011).

Challenges with communication and pragmatic skills can lead to increased negative emotions and difficulties regulating these emotions. Strategies for increasing skills in these areas are included in the Appendix.

TRAITS THAT SUPPORT EMOTION REGULATION

As we conclude this chapter, it is important to consider the traits that support effective emotion regulation. These include temperament, resilience, and emotional intelligence. As mentioned above, these traits propel a person up the proverbial ladder in order to reach their goal of emotion regulation.

Emotional Intelligence

Emotional intelligence is a subcategory of social intelligence (Salovey and Mayer 1990). Emotional intelligence has three main components: (a) the ability to monitor one's feelings and the feelings of others, (b) the ability to understand the nuances of feelings, and (c) the ability to use information regarding feelings in order to guide actions and thinking (Salovey and Mayer 1990). Goleman (1995) brought the concept of emotional intelligence into the broader public eye. The following examples illustrate some of the skills associated with emotional intelligence:

- Marta knew that Joey was sad because his grandma died. She has the ability to interpret the meaning of emotions and the interaction between emotions and relationships. (The ability to monitor one's feelings and the feelings of others.)

Chapter 2

- When Sylvia became angry with her sister, she was able to walk away to take a break so she would not say something she would regret. Sylvia has the ability to manage her emotions. She knew that taking a break would increase her positive emotions, thereby decreasing her negative emotions. (The ability to use information regarding feelings in order to guide actions and thinking.)

- Daniel broke his new toy and was able to tell his dad how furious and sad he was about breaking it. He asked for a hug. Daniel has the ability to label his emotions and recognize the different gradations of emotions. He is also able to express his emotional needs. (The ability to understand the nuances of feelings.)

The ability to monitor feelings in oneself and others, use information about feelings to guide actions and thinking, and understand the nuances of feelings are all critical components of effective emotion regulation. For more information about emotional intelligence, please refer to Diana Thompson's work at Heroes/Leaders/Champions: http://heroesleaderschampions.org/.

Temperament

Temperament refers to intrinsically based differences in emotional, motor, and attentional reactivity and the ability to self-regulate in order to adjust reactivity (Rueda and Rothbart 2009). In other words, temperament describes elements of our personality that explain how we might react to triggers, think about information, and cope with the world around us. Harvey and Penzo (2009) examined the emotional and behavioral continuum of a child who falls off a bike. This continuum ranges from the ability to talk with parents about the accident in order to receive comfort, to a child who is unable to be comforted and every level of intensity in between. This continuum is a very helpful illustration of temperament. Temperament plays a significant role in the development and effectiveness of strategies for emotion regulation.

Resilience

As discussed earlier in the positive psychology section of the book, a great deal of research has examined the role resilience plays in assisting human beings with protecting themselves against emotional challenges (Bitsika et al. 2013). Resilience is cultivated through humor; positive thinking; hopefulness; looking at things that are right, not just wrong; and recognizing the power you have over your own emotional well-being.

Henderson (2012) described the following as critical to the development and sustenance of resiliency:

- Surround yourself with people who believe you can get through tough situations ("The Resiliency Attitude").

- Focus on strengths, not challenges.

- Create caring and supportive environments ("What would I find nurturing or supportive?"); set achievable, yet high, expectations; participate and contribute; surround yourself with positive connections with people or animals; set boundaries that help you feel safe; and increase your life skills. Henderson (2012) referred to these six items as "The Resiliency Wheel."

- Recognize that building resiliency takes time and patience.

Resilience, then, paves the way for more effective emotion regulation. For specific activities and further information about resilience, please refer to Henderson's book *The Resiliency Workbook: Bounce Back Stronger, Smarter, and with Real Self-Esteem*.

SUMMARY

Chapter 2 discussed the factors, skills, and traits that facilitate more effective emotion regulation. As you reviewed the information, you probably developed a better understanding of the areas in which the children or adolescents you work with excel and struggle. The stronger children are in each of the above areas, the more likely they will develop effective emotion regulation. The appendix offers intervention ideas that will strengthen each of the skill areas.

The more children understand their emotional intelligence, temperament, and resilience, the more likely they will develop effective emotion regulation.

Chapter 2

The next chapter will help children better understand their challenges with anxiety, depression, or anger. Please remind the child that experiencing anxiety and depression does not mean they are "broken" in some way. It means they are human. Life is not easy, and there are times our feelings overwhelm us. The feelings of anxiety and depression may be the result of an identifiable life trigger like moving or a chemical predisposition toward emotional challenges. Understanding feelings and learning helpful strategies will enrich the child's life, increase positive emotions, and decrease negative feelings. An increase in positive emotions increases emotion regulation.

CHAPTER 3

THE INTERACTION BETWEEN ANXIETY, DEPRESSION, ANGER, AND EMOTION REGULATION

In this chapter, we will explore anxiety, depression, and anger. Strong emotions—positive or negative—that do not abate may indicate that the emotions have become dysregulated. Anxiety, depression, and anger are often difficult to regulate and tend to become the focus of emotion regulation interventions. Intervention strategies that fall under the umbrellas of CBT, DBT, and positive psychology are quite useful in mitigating intense anxiety, depression, and anger. They are designed to increase effective emotion regulation, which may include decreasing emotions that are intense (i.e., the child who tears apart his homework after making one spelling mistake), or increasing emotions to a more adaptive level (i.e., increasing healthy anxiety regarding an upcoming test so as to maximize performance).

As we have seen in this book (and in our lives), struggles with emotion regulation can affect social interaction, education, and employment (Geller 2005). The ability to regulate emotions is critical in that it allows for appropriate responses in social interactions and enables a person to cope with situations that are novel or changing and adjust to outside stimuli (Silk et al. 2003).

Anxiety, depression, and anger are quite prevalent in children and adolescents. These feelings are often exacerbated in children who struggle with change, social interactions, and unpredictable routines. We live in a world in which change is the norm, and social interaction requirements are complicated and ever-changing. Thus, it is critical to develop skills in the area of emotion regulation both in response to challenges with anxiety and depression and to prevent mental health challenges. It is also critical to learn emotion regulation strategies in order to minimize the "behavioral challenges" that often accompany strong emotions in children and adolescents (Silk et al. 2003). Uncontrolled emotional reactions are often mistaken for behavioral problems rather than the need to learn emotion management skills.

ANXIETY

The Diagnostic and Statistical Manual of Mental Disorders (DSM)-5 (American Psychiatric Association 2013) lists more than twenty diagnoses under the umbrella of anxiety disorders. Anxiety disorders are the most common problem facing children and adolescents (Rapee et al. 2008), affecting between 10% and 13% of children and adolescents (Chansky 2014; Rapee et al. 2008). In our post-pandemic world, these numbers are reported to have nearly doubled. It is reported that 20.5% of youth worldwide now struggle with symptoms of anxiety (DeAngelis 2022).

- Fourteen-year-old Jennifer sat in the corner of the room at her sister's birthday party. She wanted to interact with the other girls, but she did not know what to say. They were talking very quickly about boys and music. She did not know much about either topic. Facts about unicorns scrolled through her mind, and she wished she could share these facts with someone. She had been laughed at last week at her cousin's birthday party when she pretended to be a unicorn, so she thought that no matter what she did or said, she would be laughed at again. Sitting in the corner felt a lot safer than hearing kids laugh at her.

- Seven-year-old Donovan struggled with anxiety and generally found a lot of comfort in routines. This Christmas, instead of opening all of their gifts before breakfast (which was his family's routine), his parents suggested they only open one before breakfast. This change in routine increased Donovan's anxiety. In addition, he wanted a new science experiment kit, and the gift he opened was *not* a new science experiment kit. Questions and concerns rolled through his head. What if he didn't get the science experiment kit he wanted? How could his parents make him eat before he opened the rest of the gifts? Why did his mom change their routine? His mom ruined Christmas! His repetitive questions and negative thoughts increased his anxiety even more. Donovan threw himself on the floor in the middle of the family's Christmas celebration, screaming and shouting.

Chapter 3

– A QUICK NOTE ABOUT AUTISM SPECTRUM DISORDER –

As mentioned earlier, there are very high comorbidity rates of anxiety and other psychiatric disorders associated with ASD. Shaker-Naeeni et al. (2014) stated that comorbid psychiatric difficulties and ASD range from 7% to 15%. One of the biggest challenges clinicians face in assisting children with ASD is that it is difficult to make a formal diagnosis of anxiety because there are a number of diagnoses in the DSM-5, such as separation anxiety disorder, social anxiety disorder, and obsessive-compulsive and related disorders that specifically state that the symptoms must not be better described by a diagnosis of ASD. As Shaker-Naeeni et al. (2014) wrote, this seems to suggest that anxiety is a feature of ASD. Regardless of whether or not a person with ASD meets the criteria for a particular anxiety disorder, it is critical to assist children struggling with characteristics of anxiety. Interventions around anxiety disorder are particularly important given that research has shown that children with symptoms of an anxiety disorder are at higher risk for educational difficulties, unemployment, substance abuse, and other psychiatric problems (Rapee et al. 2008; Velting et al. 2004).

ANXIETY IN CHILDREN AND ADOLESCENTS

Anxiety can present differently in children and adolescents than in adults and look like "behavior problems" rather than anxiety. For example, children and adolescents with anxiety might present as defiant or rigid rather than as nervous or worried. These developmental differences may lead us down the wrong path of intervention. In other words, if a child acts in a defiant way, our interventions may be reactive or punitive in nature rather than directed at addressing the underlying anxiety. As we saw in Jennifer's and Donovan's examples above, anxiety triggered maladaptive responses that could've been interpreted as behavioral problems rather than skill deficits.

Anxiety can include physical symptoms, cognitive symptoms, and behavioral symptoms.

EMOTION REGULATION

Physical Symptoms

The physical symptoms of anxiety can include the following neurological and body reactions:

- Difficulty breathing
- Stomachaches
- Sleep disruption or trouble falling or staying asleep
- Headaches
- Fatigue
- Nausea
- Dizziness
- Unidentified illnesses
- A lump in the throat
- Tense shoulders
- Wringing hands
- Sweating
- Blushing
- Shaky legs
- Increased heart rate
- An increased urge to go to the bathroom
- Upset stomach
- Tense muscles
- A release of the chemical cortisol into the body

It is very important to help children understand what might happen in their bodies so they (a) aren't caught off-guard by the symptoms and (b) understand the fact that anxiety may be causing them to feel ill. Knowledge about the body is a step toward giving them power over their challenges.

Our physical reaction comes from a primitive response system in our body called our *fight-flight-or-freeze* system (Maack et al. 2015). Some individuals experience extreme sleepiness after a traumatic or anxiety-provoking incident as well, which is why *fall asleep* appears below. Have children imagine the following scenario:

The child walks into their bedroom and their sibling is hiding in there. Their sibling jumps out to scare them, and their body goes into fight-flight-freeze-fall asleep mode.

- **Fight:** The child punches their sibling.
- **Flight:** The child turns and runs away.
- **Freeze:** The child feels nearly paralyzed as they try to decipher what happened.
- **Fall asleep:** The stress makes the child very sleepy, and once the adrenaline wears off, the child naps.

Discuss all of the above reactions with children, and identify the reactions they think they might experience.

Fight, flight, freeze, fall asleep is a primitive response system and an important survival strategy. Unfortunately, however, anxiety can exacerbate our fight-flight-freeze-fall asleep response in such a way that the response can be more intense than we might wish, last longer than is necessary or useful, or cause more trouble than the initial trigger (e.g., punching your sister). Managing our fight-flight-freeze-fall asleep response is an important part of emotion management.

Cognitive Symptoms

We may also experience cognitive symptoms with anxiety. These symptoms include the following:

- Distorted thought patterns
- Challenges making decisions
- Difficulties concentrating
- Trouble learning new tasks

Cognitive symptoms can also include inaccurate perceptions of events, situations, or environments. For example, if someone texts us a very brief response to our text, such as "k" for "okay," and we are already experiencing anxiety, we might misperceive the short text and think the person is angry with us.

Behavioral Symptoms

It bears repeating that anxiety in children and adolescents has a sneaky way of looking like behavior problems. Although this may also be true for adults at times, the relationship between behavior problems and anxiety is more salient in children and adolescents. In reality, though, many of the "behaviors" are attempts to control the environment to lessen anxiety. Unfortunately, many of these attempts to manage the environment do not work. On the contrary, they often make the situation worse, as seen in James's meltdown and loss of privileges below.

The last time James slept at his grandparents' house, he got a migraine and vomited. His parents are going out of town, and James needs to stay with his grandparents again. He is very anxious that he will get another migraine. James's distorted thinking is, "I am going to be sick if I sleep at my grandparents' house." James refuses to walk out the door. He has a huge meltdown that worsens with each consequence set by his desperate parents. Although the consequences are not helpful or warranted, James and his parents end up in an awful cycle that includes an increase in his distress and the loss of more privileges.

Ultimately, James *has* to go to his grandparents' house, but he loses nearly all of his privileges because of his meltdown. Although the loss of privileges is not necessarily a helpful strategy for a child with emotion regulation challenges, this consequence is often used. James's inability to express his anxiety, his allegiance to his negative thinking, and his refusal to work with his parents to develop strategies made his situation worse.

The following are "behavioral" symptoms of anxiety.

- New or increased clinginess
- Challenges with separation
- Extreme shyness (that is out of character)
- Refusal or oppositional behavior
- Fidgeting
- Need for repetition, increased predictability, or rituals
- Increase or emergence of rigidity
- Unwillingness to try new things or avoidance
- Shutting down
- Hair twirling
- Hand wringing
- Nail biting
- Increased motor activity
- Repetitive questions
- Repetitive behaviors

It is helpful to know that "behaviors" such as shutting down, repetitive questions, repetitive behavior, and so on are often related to anxiety. The more children understand this relationship, the more effectively they can control their anxiety.

Explain the following to children:

It is easy to fall into the trap of believing that particular behaviors, such as avoidance or shutting down, ensure "safety." We might also believe that thinking about every possible negative event will help us avoid the negative events. All of these thoughts are distorted, however. These thoughts reinforce negative patterns that ultimately continue to fuel our anxiety rather than decrease it.

Figure 3.1 provides an example of distorted thinking.

Take a moment to reassure children. Our world is challenging right now, and

Figure 3.1: Distorted thinking

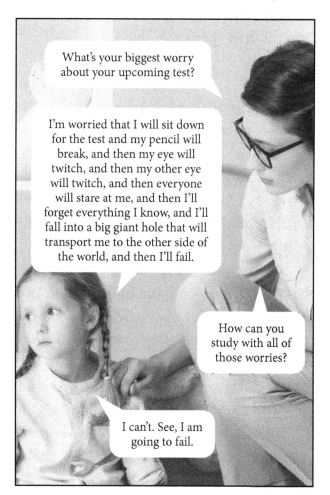

Chapter 3

my guess is that we are all experiencing a lot of anxiety. Remind children there are strategies they can use and skills they can strengthen in order to better manage anxiety. It might be helpful to go through the above "behavioral" signs of anxiety and circle the ones that are relevant to children's experiences. You can also use figure 3.2 below to help children better understand anxiety.

Figure 3.2: Worry Snowball

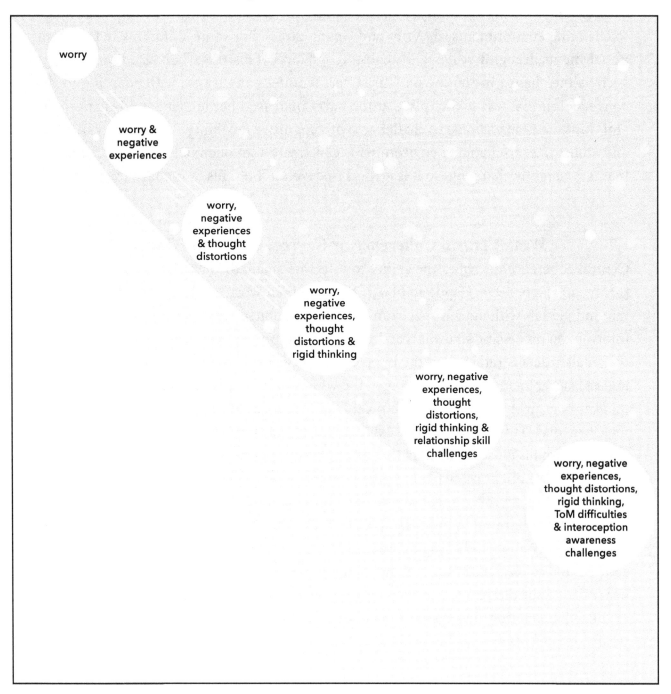

EMOTION REGULATION

CHALLENGES ASSOCIATED WITH ANXIETY

As mentioned earlier, there are a number of challenges associated with anxiety disorders in children and adolescents. I think of these challenges as future skills. As we help our children flip the following challenges into skills, their ability to manage their emotions will increase.

Cognitive Flexibility

Cognitive flexibility is the ability to switch rapidly between tasks (Monsell 2003) and adapt to changing environments (de Vries and Geurts 2012). For some children like Donovan, impairments in cognitive flexibility cause a high level of distress when faced with change, such as the change in routine on Christmas. Jennifer's challenges with adapting to the conversation that was taking place at the party increased her anxiety and isolation. Literal thinking is an example of challenges with cognitive flexibility. The inability to adapt and adjust to ever-changing environments can create a lot of anxiety. We live in a world that is constantly changing, so it is critical to develop the skills to manage this reality.

Weak Central Coherence or Central Coherence Theory

Central coherence describes the ability to integrate small, distinct elements into a whole (Frith and Happé 1994; Happé and Frith 2006). In their work, Frith and Happé postulated that individuals with autism spectrum disorders exhibited weak central coherence or an information processing style that can lead to misinterpretation of cues because of focus on the smaller details rather than the big picture. Focusing on small (and potentially meaningless) variables rather than looking at the whole body of information can cause anxiety (Shaker-Naeeni et al. 2014). For example, Donovan focused so intently on the change in the Christmas Day schedule that he could not assimilate the fact that he would still be able to open all of his gifts. His anxiety that he might not get one particular gift overshadowed the fact that he might receive other gifts he wanted. Jennifer's focus on her fears that she would not have anything to contribute to a conversation about boys or music caused her anxiety and withdrawal to increase. If, instead, Jennifer thought about the fact that listening in a conversation and engaging was as important, if not more important, than offering content to a conversation, she may have attempted to join the girls. This may have led to her realizing she did have something to contribute to the conversation after all.

Effective emotion management requires assessment and understanding of both the small components and the big picture.

Chapter 3

Cognitive Distortions

Cognitive distortions describe the automatic assumptions and thoughts we have about ourselves and/or situations (Burns 1989). These automatic assumptions and thoughts are typically irrational or exaggerated in nature. Cognitive distortions can lead to negative thinking, which can influence our mood. The tendency to think in a very literal manner and approach the world with a rather rigid set of views and beliefs can lead to cognitive distortions, which can increase anxiety. For example, Jennifer thought her sister's friends would laugh at her if she tried to talk with them. Although this may have happened in the past because she pretended to be a unicorn, this would not necessarily happen again by simply interacting with peers. Jennifer's distorted thinking led her to stay in the corner and avoid any interaction at all, thus increasing her social anxiety and negative feelings.

Challenges with Relationship Skills

Challenges with relationship skills and a history of negative social interaction can lead to an increase in anxiety (Bellini 2016; Bellini 2006; Reaven et al. 2012). When children experience repetitive rejection and/or engage in ineffective attempts at meaningful social interactions, anxiety can increase.

Sensory Challenges

Kerns and Kendall (2013) discussed their review of the literature that examines the interaction between sensory challenges and anxiety. Kerstein (2008) examined the relationship between sensory integration dysfunction or sensory processing disorder and an increase in characteristics of anxiety. These examinations found an inextricable relationship between sensory issues and anxiety. The bombardment of sensory triggers and ineffective management of these triggers can be very stressful for children.

Chemicals and the Brain

A number of chemicals are also associated with anxiety. These chemical or neurological influences can include serotonin, gamma-aminobutyric acid (GABA), and corticotropin-releasing hormone (Wicks-Nelson and Israel 2009). In addition, anxiety has genetic influences. It is important to examine these variables in order to determine the most appropriate and effective model of treatment for a child struggling with anxiety.

EMOTION REGULATION

DEPRESSION

Depression describes a state of feeling sad, dejected, or despondent.

Twenty-year-old Asher really wants a girlfriend. Many of the people on his soccer team in college have begun dating, and he feels left out. He has been on a few dates with women, but they usually do not go very well. In fact, the last date was a disaster. During the date, a person came up to talk with his date, and Asher misread the person's cues. He thought the person was hitting on his date and lost control of his feelings. He ended up getting into a screaming match with the person, and his date walked away. Asher realizes he does not know how to manage his feelings very well, and he gets very discouraged about this.

– A QUICK NOTE ABOUT AUTISM SPECTRUM DISORDER –

Characteristics of depression and other mood disorders, such as bipolar disorders and disruptive mood dysregulation disorder, are often exhibited in individuals with ASD (Matson and Williams 2014). As Matson and Williams stated, it is important to identify any potential comorbid challenges associated with a diagnosis of ASD so interventions can begin as quickly as possible.

Contributing Factors

Difficulties with executive function—particularly cognitive flexibility, weak central coherence, cognitive distortions, challenges with relationship skills, and sensory challenges play a significant role in the development of characteristics of depression.

Depression and anxiety have a high comorbidity rate, sharing such core features as negative affect and general distress (Hranov 2007). It is important to note that the research identifies hopelessness (or a feeling that life events will not go as desired) as unique to depression (Beck et al. 2006). Although interventions specific to hopelessness are not specifically discussed in this book, CBT is one of the strategies often used to work with children experiencing hopelessness. In addition to the chemical, neurological, and genetic components associated with depression, some people encounter challenges that trigger characteristics of depression. They may have expressed feelings of hopelessness, frustration, and intense sadness over the struggles they have socially, academically, and with the sensory world. Students with challenges such as ADHD, ASD, or learning challenges may feel depressed because they feel like they are different from their peers. In Asher's case, he recognizes he is different and struggling, but does not know what to do about it.

Chapter 3

– LEARNED HELPLESSNESS AND ANXIETY, DEPRESSION, AND ANGER –

Learned helplessness is an important concept to review when thinking about the hopelessness associated with depression. Learned helplessness occurs when people believe their actions do not affect the outcome of a situation, problem, or challenge (Abramson et al. 1978; Peterson 2006). For example, Juan, a first grader, struggles with undiagnosed dyslexia. He has tried very hard to learn to read with little success. Since Juan's hard work has yet to change the outcome, he is ready to give up.

Children like Juan typically explain negative events as something outside of their control, in a *negative explanatory style* (Peterson 2006). This explanatory style or attributional style affects the amount of control a person perceives he has over future events. In reality, with the right type of support, such as learning strategies and skill training, Juan could have an impact on the outcome of future events with regard to reading. Juan, with the help of an adult, may switch from pessimism, helplessness, and hopelessness to a more optimistic style of thinking.

The development of optimism comes from the ability to flip thinking, evaluate the accuracy of negative thoughts, develop the ability to look at both the reality and the possibilities at the same time, think like a wizard (problem-solve), and identify ways in which we *do* have control over a situation. In doing these things, we can avoid the paralysis, depression, anxiety, and anger that often come with learned helplessness.

Presentation in Children and Adolescents

Depression can also present differently in children and adolescents than in adults. This presentation might include but is not limited to the symptoms described in table 3.1:

Table 3.1: POSSIBLE CHARACTERISTICS OF DEPRESSION

- Complaints of feeling sick
- School refusal
- Refusal to attend social functions
- Increased neediness or clinginess
- Extreme worry about such issues as a parent dying or things going wrong
- Increased trouble at school
- Feelings of irritability
- Feelings of isolation
- An increase in sleeping or a change in eating patterns
- Increased crying
- Disinterest in activities that were previously enjoyed (Briers 2009; Chansky 2008)

EMOTION REGULATION

Take a moment to locate table 3.1 in the Appendix so you may go through the characteristics of depression listed above with the child. Circle or discuss those that may apply to the child. It is very important for children to receive help from a professional skilled in the area of depression (or continued help from you) if they are struggling.

ANGER

Challenges with emotion regulation can lead to an increase in anger. After all, if a person has difficulties understanding and regulating emotions, such as sadness, frustration, and disappointment, the presentation of these emotions could emerge as anger. In addition, as mentioned earlier, research has shown that children and adolescents often express anxiety and depression very differently than adults. At times, this expression can look like anger and include meltdowns/tantrums or aggressive behavior (Rapee et al. 2008). It is very important, then, to intervene and support children struggling with anger. Given challenges in the area of emotion regulation, anger can quickly become an area of great concern if not addressed.

It is important to note that children experiencing difficulties, such as ADHD, ASD, anxiety, depression, anger, and learning challenges, are also more likely to be victims of bullying (Rieffe et al. 2012). This can cause children to feel anger as well as extreme distress and trauma.

– IMPORTANT NOTE –

If you are a teacher or therapist and are in any way concerned that a child might hurt themselves or others, please know and follow the plan for responding to such concerns in your workplace. If you are the child's caregiver and are concerned, please seek professional help. It is critical to help the child connect with a clinician who is trained to address their needs. SAFETY ALWAYS COMES FIRST! Although this book will help with feelings of depression, sadness, and anger, it is critical to ensure the child or adolescent is SAFE FIRST by asking specific questions about self-harm or harm of others, coordinating with caregivers, and enlisting outside support as needed.

NEXT STEPS: EXAMINING SPECIFIC INTERVENTION STRATEGIES

In the past decade, huge advancements have taken place in terms of addressing anxiety, depression, and anger. These advancements have included the use of CBT, DBT, and

Chapter 3

positive psychology. The next few chapters look at these models of intervention and offer specific strategies that might be helpful in reducing anxiety, depression, and anger in children and adolescents.

The overarching theme in each of the intervention models and subsequent strategies is that once children identify (triggers, feelings, intensity), design (helpful strategies), educate (themselves about when to use the strategies) and actively use intervention strategies, they will increase their ability to manage their emotions.

The regulation of emotions is quite complex. It is like adjusting a thermostat that is unique to each individual child and each specific situation. For some children, regulating emotions may mean increasing positive emotions (i.e., enjoying a positive experience), while for others, it may mean decreasing positive emotions so that they are more manageable (i.e., modulating joy so that children can function in a classroom setting safely). For other children, regulating emotions might mean increasing negative emotions (i.e., reacting with anxiety to a dangerous situation), or decreasing negative emotions (i.e., learning to decrease anxiety in order to try a new experience).

The intent of the interventions described in the following chapters is to provide tools for regulating emotions, not to suggest that we need to rid ourselves of emotions. Feeling is human. There are times when it is important to sit with emotion, such as in grief, and allow ourselves to feel.

The strategies listed in the following chapters will assist children in the development of an IDEA action plan:

- **Identify** triggers, feelings, and intensity.

- **Design** emotion regulation strategies.

- **Educate** children about the specific situations in which the strategies might be most helpful. Teach and rehearse strategies to ensure they know how to carry them out effectively.

- **Actively** model, support, and encourage the use of intervention strategies to increase children's ability to regulate their emotions. Set up systems that reinforce the use of strategies so as to increase children's motivation and success.

EMOTION REGULATION

For example:

Liat, a second grader, consistently asks to go to the school nurse for headaches and stomachaches. She usually rests for a few minutes and then feels ready to return to class. The nurse asked the school social worker to talk with Liat to assess whether or not anxiety is playing a role in her medical complaints. The school social worker spoke with Liat, who said it helps her stomachaches and headaches to rest in the nurse's office for a little while. She said she sometimes has big feelings in the classroom that make her head and stomach hurt. The school social worker then asked the teacher to try to identify the specific circumstances surrounding Liat's requests to go to the nurse. After a week of tracking information, the teacher realized that Liat asks to go to the nurse directly following moments when the room becomes loud or disorganized (at a transition, for example). The school social worker worked with Liat to do the following:

- **Identify** the specific trigger that might cause the headaches and stomachaches. Liat was able to recognize that the disorganization and noise bothered her ears. Liat and the school social worker talked about the feelings of fear that Liat felt when her ears hurt. They also investigated the intensity of this fear by rating it with a circle scale, as indicated below in figure 3.3:

Figure 3.3: Circle rating

A tiny circle represented a very small amount of fear, a medium circle represented a medium amount of fear, and a large circle represented a huge amount of fear.

- **Design** strategies to help her when she is triggered. The school social worker then helped Liat create a toolbox of strategies for the noise, which included earplugs and an "I need a break" ticket that gave Liat permission to walk to the water fountain to get a drink of water while the class transitioned.

- **Educate** Liat about times when her toolbox might be most helpful. Liat, with the help of the social worker, made a list and drew pictures to identify the times during the day when the toolbox might be most helpful. They rehearsed and role-played these strategies during times when Liat was calm and regulated.

- **Actively** model and encourage Liat to use her strategies. The teacher and school social worker set up a reinforcement system that actively supported Liat each time she identified and engaged a strategy.

Although there were times Liat still asked to go to the nurse, the frequency of these requests decreased significantly. As you read the additional intervention strategies throughout this book, keep IDEA in mind.

SUMMARY

The next chapter reviews specific intervention strategies that will help children develop more effective emotion regulation strategies. Each of the strategies is rooted in CBT, DBT, and positive psychology. As you review the strategies, it is important to remember that emotion regulation is an ongoing process. There are times when regulating emotions is easier than others. New life challenges can both positively and negatively impact a person's ability to regulate. It is helpful to have a toolbox of strategies available at all times. It is also helpful to remember that individualizing strategies is most useful, as each child or adolescent's needs are quite varied and diverse.

CHAPTER 4
ADDITIONAL INTERVENTION STRATEGIES TO SUPPORT EMOTION REGULATION

Intervention strategies that help children regulate their emotions are sprinkled throughout the first three chapters. This chapter focuses on additional interventions that can help children manage emotions. The more interventions you add to a child's toolbox, the more successful they will be.

All of the intervention strategies incorporate CBT, DBT, and/or positive psychology strategies. The goal of these interventions is to increase emotion management skills.

Remember, as we saw with Liat, we are trying to increase our children's IDEAs about how to help themselves regulate their emotions. IDEA includes:

- **Identify** triggers, feelings, and intensity.

- **Design** emotion regulation strategies.

- **Education** about the specific situations in which the strategies might be most helpful. Teach and rehearse strategies to ensure the child knows how to carry them out effectively.

- **Actively** model, support, and encourage the use of intervention strategies to increase the child's ability to regulate their emotions. Set up systems that reinforce the use of strategies so as to increase the child's motivation and success.

Please keep the information below in mind (as was discussed in previous chapters) as you work through the intervention strategies with children.

EMOTION REGULATION

1. **Triggers:** A trigger is something that causes an action or reaction. Triggers play a huge role in impacting both positive and negative emotional reactions. The better children understand the concept of a trigger and the things that trigger them, the more equipped they will be to handle their emotional responses.

2. **Fight, flight, freeze, fall asleep:** Our system of fight, flight, freeze, fall asleep is an important, primitive system that can be protective in nature. This system keeps us safe in the face of danger (e.g., staying away from a swerving car, avoiding a dangerous situation, or standing up in the face of a bully). Anxiety, however, can exacerbate our fight-flight-freeze-fall asleep response in challenging ways. The reaction might be more intense than necessary for the situation, last longer than is helpful, or cause more trouble than the initial trigger (e.g., running from a teacher who is trying to help you because you are afraid of getting in trouble). Modulating our fight-flight-freeze-fall asleep responses is a part of emotion management.

3. **Strengths:** In order to manage feelings effectively, it is critical to recognize our strengths and build on them.

4. **Thought patterns:** It is important to help children recognize their thought patterns (both negative and positive). We can work on changing negative patterns of thoughts and increasing positive thoughts in order to take control of our feelings.

LEARN HOW TO READ YOURSELF TO BE READY

In order to regulate emotions, children must first know how to read their feelings, triggers, core beliefs, assumptions, and fight-flight-freeze-fall asleep response; assess the intensity of their emotions; and then implement strategies that help them feel READY to take charge of their feelings.

Mindfulness

One of the ways to help children READ themselves better is to work on mindfulness. The following activities might help children increase their ability to be mindful. Examples are provided below in figure 4.1. A blank worksheet can be found in the appendix or online.

Chapter 4

Figure 4.1: Pause! Notice Your Surroundings *(Example)*

Take a moment to notice the details around you. Don't analyze them, judge them, or formulate a response of any sort. Just notice! What do you see? Hear? Smell? Taste? What are you touching? Where are you? How does your body feel? What emotions are you experiencing?

Take a moment to write them down or talk through them:

 I see my dad making dinner in the kitchen.

 I feel the bumpy ridges of blocks in my hands.

 I smell onions.

 I taste the peppermint gum in my mouth.

 I hear the sizzle, sizzle, pop of the onions in the frying pan.

 I am sitting on the rug in our family room, leaning up against the couch.

 I feel nervous that I might not like dinner.

EMOTION REGULATION

As you talk through the observations children made, expand upon this new mindfulness by focusing on particular details of each observation.

Snapshot

Walk with children and pick a particular moment to snapshot, for example, a bird chirping on a high branch of a tree. Encourage children to focus on every detail of a particular moment and consciously say to themselves, "I'm going to remember this moment." This activity will help children work on mindfulness.

Rubber Band Brain

Talk with children about our brains being like rubber band brains. Our thoughts might wander for a moment—much like the stretching of a rubber band—but then we need to consciously snap them back into place in order to fully attend to the task.

For more information about increasing mindfulness in children, visit http://mindfullifetoday.com/mindfulness-programs/.

Feelings

Feelings can be **short and fleeting**, **mild**, or **intense**. Feelings can **come and go** like waves in the ocean or **linger** like an itch from a mosquito bite. When emotions linger—the itch that keeps on itching—they can become quite difficult to manage. For example, Malia's dog passed away. Her grief and sadness impacted her ability to focus in school. She was not only sad about losing her dog, she was worried other important people or pets would pass away too. Her feelings of sadness and worry have lingered and are affecting her daily life. Her feelings have also remained intense, which has made emotion regulation difficult.

Understanding feelings is a skill. It is important to make sure our children understand feelings before proceeding with the rest of the strategies outlined in this chapter. Try the following activities with children in order to teach them about feelings.

1. **Feeling collage:** Gather magazines and cut pictures out of different-feeling faces. Make a collage of the feelings you discover.

2. **Feeling books:** Make a book series with children. Create a book about each feeling.

3. **Videos:** Watch video clips of sitcoms, videos, or television shows. Discuss the feelings you see. Play a game where you challenge each other to write down every

feeling you see in a given scene. You can even watch the scenes with the sound off to challenge yourself to identify emotions based on visual/nonverbal information only.

4. **Bodies:** Draw a picture of the outline of a body. Help children identify the places in their body where they feel certain emotions. For example, a child may say they feel worry in their stomach because it feels like butterflies are fluttering around.

5. **Faces:** Practice acting out different feelings. Accentuate the different parts of your face or body that express feelings. For example, your eyebrows may curve down, your lips tighten, your arms cross, and your muscles tighten when angry.

Read Yourself to Be READY

Once children have a better understanding of feelings, you can begin to explore triggers, core beliefs, assumptions, the fight-flight-freeze-fall asleep response, intensity, and thoughts. The READY acronym can be very helpful in helping children understand and address their emotional regulation:

- **RECOGNIZE** triggers, core beliefs, and assumptions.

- **EVALUATE** fight-flight-freeze-fall asleep response and lizard thinking.

- **ASSESS** the intensity of emotions.

- **DIRECT** thoughts and emotions to a place that is more manageable.

- **YOUR CHILDREN ARE** stronger than their feelings. They can be in charge of their feelings and emotions.

Although this book reads in a linear way, this process is not linear at all. Exploring all of the different components associated with emotion regulation requires flexibility (i.e., thinking with your wizard brain), as you will need to help children move back and forth between different skills in order to understand the relationship between triggers, feelings, thoughts, and behaviors or actions.

EMOTION REGULATION

RECOGNIZE TRIGGERS, CORE BELIEFS, AND ASSUMPTIONS

Creating a Better Understanding of Triggers

Triggers are tricky. They can cause negative feelings, positive feelings, or both. Additionally, triggers can be internal (a cold) or external (a bad grade). As you work with children on the identification of triggers, it is helpful to point out the difference between internal triggers and external triggers.

Remind children that triggers cause us to think thoughts that can be positive or negative. Those thoughts lead to emotions and behaviors or actions. Share figure 4.2 below with the child or adolescent to illustrate this relationship.

Figure 4.2: Thoughts, feelings, actions

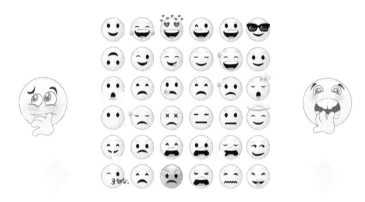

Thoughts, feelings, and actions can be further explored using the following two examples.

1. **Trigger:** Finals are two days away.
   Thought: Michelle thinks she'll fail.
   Feeling: Panic
   Behavior/action: She has a full-blown tantrum and throws her study guides across the room.

   OR

2. **Trigger:** It begins to rain.
   Thought: Deja thinks about the plants and how much they need this rain.
   Feeling: Thrilled
   Behavior/action: Deja dances around the room.

You can challenge your child to reverse each of these scenarios with you to see how the outcomes change.

Chapter 4

– A QUICK NOTE ABOUT AUTISM SPECTRUM DISORDER –

Many children on the autism spectrum have told me they do not feel emotions the same way others seem to feel them. It is entirely possible that even basic emotions are more of a learned experience for children on the spectrum. In assisting children with ASD, we must recognize there isn't a prescriptive way to feel sadness or happiness or other emotions. Each person feels these emotions in different ways, because of varying triggers, and at disparate levels of intensity. Despite these unique experiences, it is my theory that learning about and understanding emotions in others and ourselves is critical in order to manage emotions in our everyday lives. One way to examine the different emotional experiences children might have is to watch clips of sitcoms or other television shows together.

First, watch the clip with the sound off. Encourage children to predict what feelings the characters are experiencing. Look at the triggers, intensity of the feelings, and strategies the characters use. Then rewind and watch the clip with the sound on. Were the children's assumptions correct? Watching people experience feelings in a nonthreatening environment, such as a sitcom, can shed light on individual differences in emotion processing.

Exploring Triggers

Remind children about the relationship between triggers, feelings, behaviors, or actions and the possible result of these actions. Use figure 4.3 below to help you explain this relationship:

Figure 4.3: From trigger to action

A trigger happens.

Thoughts pop into your mind as you perceive the event.
(Note: These perceptions and thoughts may or may not be accurate!)

Your thoughts and perceptions cause feelings.

Your feelings cause actions.
(Negative thoughts or perceptions often lead to negative actions.)

EMOTION REGULATION

The following example illustrates this sequence by showing two ways a person might think, feel, and act in a particular situation. This diagram also shows the different results that occur depending on the person's reaction.

Figure 4.4 illustrates the power that positive, accurate thoughts (and wizard thinking) have in facilitating the effective management of feelings and actions.

Figure 4.4: One trigger, two responses

Event/Trigger

Event/Trigger

Thought:
"I am a total idiot. I always make mistakes. I probably just ruined my keyboard."

Thought:
"I made a mistake, which happens sometimes. I am sure there are ways to dry my keyboard quickly so it will be okay."

Feeling:
Sad, anxious, angry, defeated

Feeling:
Frustrated, hopeful, a bit nervous

Action:
Cry, scream, throw keyboard, throw hot chocolate mug

Action:
Pick up the hot chocolate mug, turn the keyboard upside down to let the liquid run out, Google "What should I do if I spill liquid on my keyboard?"

Result:
The keyboard and mug are completely broken. You have a sore throat from screaming.

Result:
Your keyboard dries out and works well. You refill your hot chocolate and set it ten feet from your keyboard.

Triggers (Negative)

Use the following scale to help children rate each trigger to determine whether it would bother or impact them negatively. Please remind children that everyone is different and experiences different triggers and different emotional reactions to situations!

Chapter 4

Table 4.1: NEGATIVE TRIGGERS

Name: _____   Date: _____

Directions: Circle the number that describes the degree of intensity of the trigger in each situation.
   1 = small trigger;   2 = medium trigger;   3 = big trigger

Situation			
Being invited to a party	1	2	3
Hearing a loud noise	1	2	3
Someone not believing you	1	2	3
Your friend not being able to hang out	1	2	3
The smell of certain foods	1	2	3
A new challenge	1	2	3
Being left out when other people are together	1	2	3
Doing poorly on a test	1	2	3
Someone yelling (not necessarily at you)	1	2	3
Missing your favorite show	1	2	3
Being out of your favorite food	1	2	3
Bright lights	1	2	3
Having a cold	1	2	3
Feeling out of control because someone else is being bossy	1	2	3
Making a mistake	1	2	3
Feeling unsure what to do because you're in a new place	1	2	3
People being mean to you	1	2	3
Getting hurt	1	2	3
Needing food because you're hungry	1	2	3
Not getting enough sleep	1	2	3
Something bad happening	1	2	3
Your birthday	1	2	3
Being told to put away something you don't want to	1	2	3

EMOTION REGULATION

Triggers (Positive)

There are also triggers that can cause us to feel positive feelings. Help children think about each of the triggers listed in table 4.2 on the next page.

You will notice that some items from the previous table appear on this list also because the same triggers can be negative for some and positive for others. Determine whether the triggers would cause children to feel a positive feeling and to what degree, using the same 0–3 scale. Remind children that everyone is different and has unique triggers and variable emotional reactions to situations, and that is okay!

Tricky Triggers (Positive and Negative)

As you discussed the triggers with children, you may have noticed that some cause negative *and* positive emotions. I call these *tricky* triggers. Explain to children that it is helpful to examine all the details in our environments. As we increase our ability to perceive all the different environmental variables, we can better understand the way tricky triggers impact our feelings. Understanding our surroundings can assist us with accurately **reading** ourselves.

Vermeulen (2012) talks about context. Context provides us with historical information, situational information, location, or information about what we hear, see, smell, touch, or experience in the present moment. You may explain it to a child like this:

> Seeing our favorite video game might trigger us to feel happy, unless that video game is on someone else's device and we can't play it. The context—someone else's device—changes our reaction to the trigger. The context of a particular situation (e.g., those around us, the way we are feeling, how much sleep we got last night, and what we see, hear, or smell) can change the impact a trigger might have on our feelings, thoughts, and behaviors.

Please take a moment to look at the triggers listed in table 4.3: Tricky Triggers (on pages 56–57) and let's review it together. It is helpful to think about the components of the situation or context that increase or decrease potential triggers for you. You may even want to think about the whys—why something might bother you more in a particular situation or less in a different situation. Tricky triggers can cause us to feel opposite emotions, depending on the context.

Chapter 4

Table 4.2: POSITIVE TRIGGERS

Name: _____   Date: _____

Directions: Circle the number that describes the degree of intensity of the trigger in each situation.
1 = small trigger;   2 = medium trigger;   3 = big trigger

Situation	Small	Medium	Big
Being invited to a party	1	2	3
Spending time with a friend	1	2	3
Seeing your mom	1	2	3
Seeing your dad	1	2	3
Your birthday	1	2	3
Drinking your favorite drink	1	2	3
Eating your favorite food	1	2	3
Being at the beach	1	2	3
Reading a good book	1	2	3
Listening to music	1	2	3
People being treated fairly	1	2	3
Someone being kind to you	1	2	3
Feeling healthy	1	2	3
Dancing	1	2	3
Singing	1	2	3
A sunny day	1	2	3
Gaming	1	2	3
Watching a movie	1	2	3
Having extra time to spend with your hobbies or interests	1	2	3

EMOTION REGULATION

Table 4.3: TRICKY TRIGGERS

Name: _____   Date: _____

Triggers	This Is Harder When ...	This Would Not Bother Me as Much When ...
Hearing a loud noise	This is harder for me when I am in an unfamiliar situation because I am not always sure what the noise is, so it scares me more.	This would not bother me as much when it is expected, like at a concert, because it is usually easier for me to figure out what the noise is so I don't become as scared.
Someone not believing you	This is difficult for me in most situations.	I think this would bother me in all situations.
Your friend not being able to hang out	I would be upset about this, especially if I felt particularly lonely that day.	I wouldn't be as upset about this if I had other things to do that I enjoyed.
The smell of certain foods		
A new challenge		
Being left out when other people are together		
Doing poorly on a test		
Someone yelling (not necessarily at you)		
Missing your favorite show		
Being out of your favorite food		
Bright lights		
Having a cold		
Feeling out of control because someone is being bossy		
Making a mistake		

Chapter 4

Being unsure of what to do because you are in a new place

People being mean to you

Getting hurt

Needing food because you're hungry

Not getting enough sleep

Something bad happening

Your birthday

Being invited to a party

Spending time with a friend

Seeing your mom

Seeing your dad

Drinking your favorite drink

Eating your favorite food

Being at the beach

Reading a good book

People being treated fairly

Someone being kind to you

Feeling healthy

Dancing

Singing

A sunny day

Gaming

Watching a movie

EMOTION REGULATION

Map Out Your Triggers and Feelings

Take a moment to examine the relationship between triggers and feelings. Try the following with children:

1. Help the child or adolescent select three triggers from the previous lists, or three other triggers they recognize in their life. You might need to share your observations regarding triggers the child has described.

2. Write the triggers in the center square of the diagram in the Appendix (p. 128).

3. Write or draw a picture of the feelings the child typically experiences when faced with each trigger. The feelings might be positive or negative.

4. Write down the place where the child typically feels the feeling (in mind/thoughts, body i.e., chest, stomach, stiffness of muscles, head).

5. Take a moment to help the child recognize that it is **okay** to have every feeling you wrote down together.

As you complete this activity, it is critical to acknowledge that we have feelings, and we cannot always exhibit perfect control (Linehan 1993). We want to help our children understand that they will not always have control over the feelings that arise. It is important to help our children give themselves permission to feel feelings rather than judge or criticize themselves for having feelings in the first place. Triggers can cause our children (and all of us, for that matter) to feel rotten, elated, sad, happy, anxious, overjoyed, angry, loving, and everything in between. We want our children or adolescents to understand that it is what they do with these feelings that ultimately matters. Figure 4.5 on the next page illustrates this:

Chapter 4

Figure 4.5: Triggered responses

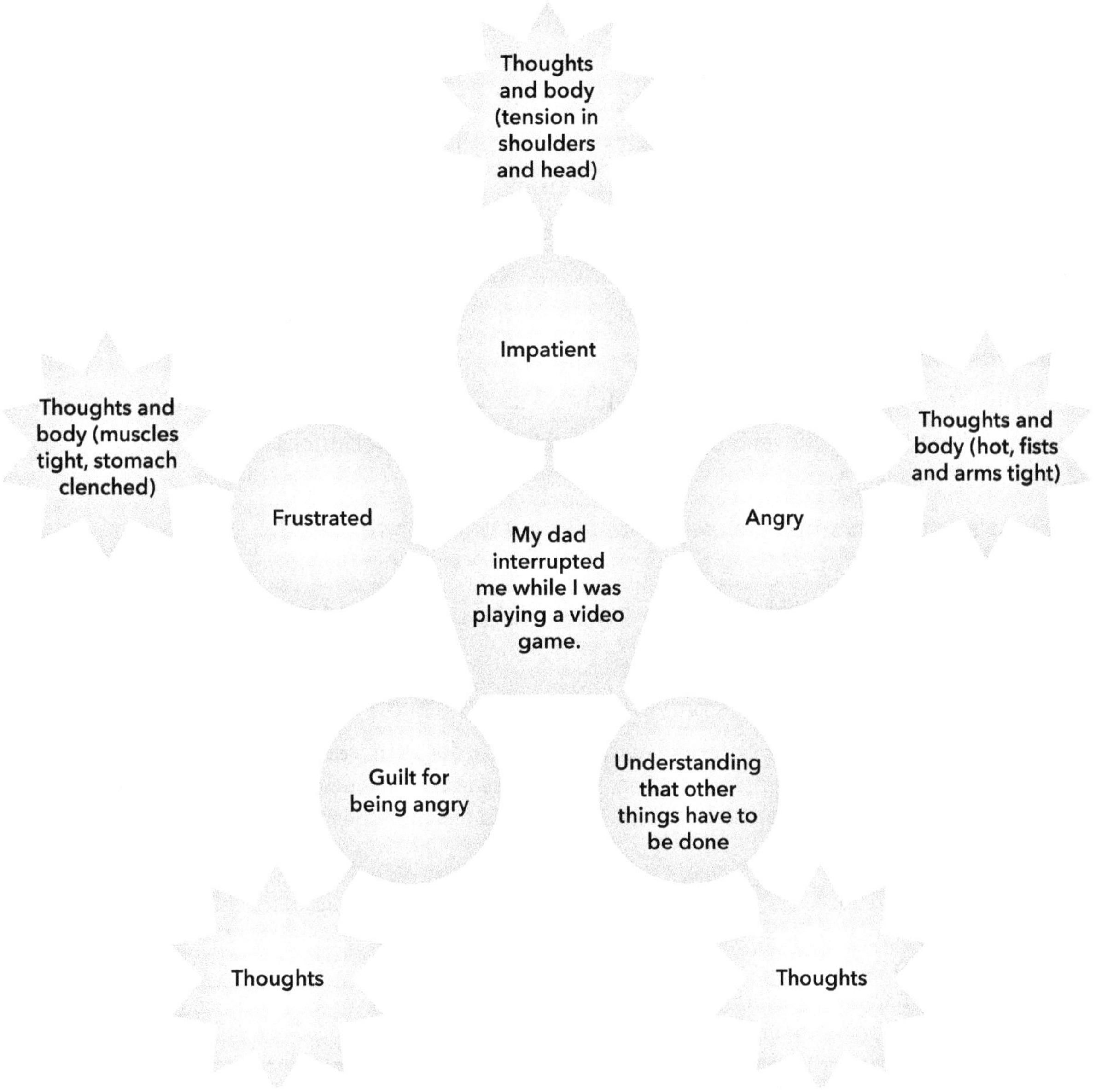

Center: My dad interrupted me while I was playing a video game.

- **Impatient** — Thoughts and body (tension in shoulders and head)
- **Frustrated** — Thoughts and body (muscles tight, stomach clenched)
- **Angry** — Thoughts and body (hot, fists and arms tight)
- **Guilt for being angry** — Thoughts
- **Understanding that other things have to be done** — Thoughts

EMOTION REGULATION

Now take a moment to try this activity with the child or adolescent. You can use three of the triggers the child may have identified when you discussed positive, negative, and tricky triggers.

It is amazing how many triggers we experience in a given day. As described earlier, these triggers can range from internal triggers, such as being hungry, to external triggers, such as an interruption. The more awareness children develop around triggers and the feelings they can cause, the better they can manage their emotions or feelings.

Increasing Positive Experiences

As mentioned, triggers are not always negative. They can also cause **positive** feelings, positive core beliefs, and positive assumptions. Help children identify positive triggers. Positive triggers will assist children with managing their emotions. Positive triggers and experiences are like the oil for children's "cars." The more children can add positive experiences and triggers to their lives, the better their lives will feel and the more manageable emotions will be!

Note: For some children, positive emotions are difficult to regulate as well. It is important to recognize this in children so you can select positive experiences that will be supportive rather than dysregulating.

Please see the example below before filling it out with the child.

Figure 4.6: Positive Experience Plan

Name: _____   Date: _____

I plan to add the following experiences to my life in order to increase my positive feelings. (These experiences could be swinging on a swing, a trip to the library, riding a bike, taking a walk, reading a favorite book, drawing, or anything that helps the child feel more positive.):

1. Take a walk
2. Read a magazine
3. Listen to music
4. _____
5. _____

Chapter 4

What Has Gone "Right?"

Additionally, the more children recognize the things that have gone "right" each day, the more positive feelings they will have. Take a moment to talk about things that are going well.

Core Beliefs and Assumptions

Our *core beliefs* are the basic assumptions we make about ourselves, which cause us to have automatic thoughts. Core beliefs include the way we see ourselves, the judgments we make about ourselves, and our view of the future (Stallard 2002). Core beliefs cause us to see ourselves a certain way and therefore affect our feelings. Teaching children about core beliefs will help them manage their emotions. You can teach core beliefs through the following activities.

X-Ray Machine

Ask children: If the mirror was like an x-ray machine and you could look inside yourself, what would you see? What beliefs do you have about yourself? Figure 4.7 below offers examples of possible core beliefs children may have. The examples show both positive and negative core beliefs. Take a moment to locate a blank figure 4.7 X-Ray Machine worksheet in the appendix and fill it out with children.

Figure 4.7: X-Ray Machine

Name: _____   Date: _____

1. I am: **a hard worker.**

2. I can: **lose my temper easily.**

3. I always: **freak out**

4. I wish I: **could stay calm.**

5. People think I'm: **shy**

EMOTION REGULATION

Mirror

You can also work with children to identify core beliefs through figure 4.8: Look in the Mirror.

Figure 4.8: Look in the Mirror

Name: _____   Date: _____

When you look in the mirror, what do you see? I see: <u>A person who is terrible at sports.</u>

How much do you like what you see?   0   1   2   3   4   5

When you look in the mirror, what do you see? I see: <u>A person who is really good at playing the violin.</u>

How much do you like what you see?   0   1   2   3   4   5

When you look in the mirror, what do you see? I see: _____

How much do you like what you see?   0   1   2   3   4   5

When you look in the mirror, what do you see? I see: _____

How much do you like what you see?   0   1   2   3   4   5

When you look in the mirror, what do you see? I see: _____

How much do you like what you see?   0   1   2   3   4   5

After the child fills this out, ask them to think about where those core beliefs come from. For example, when I was in sixth grade, my art teacher told me something to the effect of, "Make sure you don't plan a career in art." Not surprisingly, I developed a core belief that I was a terrible artist and should not plan to draw at all throughout my life. Ironically, I ended up in a career in which I often draw for and with my clients. It has taken a lot of work to have confidence in my drawings, accept the level of skill I have, and draw without my nagging core belief getting in the way.

Does the child have any core beliefs they want to quiet? Work with the child to fill out table 4.4: Origin of Core Beliefs. Together you and the child can identify where their core

Chapter 4

beliefs came from and ways to counteract these core beliefs so they don't affect the child and create anxiety. Conversely, you can also identify positive core beliefs that help the child regulate more effectively.

Table 4.4: ORIGIN OF CORE BELIEFS

Name: _____   Date: _____

Core belief	I think this started when …
I am a terrible artist.	This belief started when my sixth-grade art teacher told me I should plan a career that does not include art.
I am a compassionate person.	I think this started when I was a very young girl and used to identify strongly with the emotions of the characters I read in books.

Once the child identifies their core beliefs, take a moment to think about assumptions they might make as a result of their core beliefs. Examples are provided in table 4.5: Core Beliefs and Assumptions.

As you can see, some core beliefs and assumptions can be quite helpful, while others can be rather destructive. As a result, core beliefs and assumptions can lead to positive or negative emotions.

Practice identifying core beliefs and assumptions with children by filling out table 4.5: Core Beliefs and Assumptions, which can be found in the appendix and online.

EMOTION REGULATION

Table 4.5: CORE BELIEFS AND ASSUMPTIONS

Name: _____   Date: _____

Core belief	Assumption
I am not very good at talking with a group of people in social situations.	IF I am not good at talking with a group of people in social situations, THEN I will never make friends.
I am very good at remembering facts.	IF I am good at remembering facts, THEN I will do well on a multiple-choice test.
I am stupid.	IF I am stupid, THEN I will fail this test.
I am caring.	IF I am caring, THEN I will be cared about by other people.

Now that you have helped the child identify their core beliefs, from where they originated, and the assumptions they make as a result, take a moment to think about the impact core beliefs have on the child's life. You may find examples of the impact core beliefs may have on a person's life in table 4.6: Impact of Core Beliefs (on the next page). Table 4.6 can be found in the appendix and online so you may explore this with the child.

Identifying strengths will help the child challenge their core beliefs and assumptions. Examples of this can be found on the next page in table 4.7: Find my Strengths to Challenge Assumptions. You can also find table 4.7 in the appendix and online. Take a moment to work within the positive psychology framework and help children identify strengths.

Core beliefs can affect the way we feel about ourselves, assumptions we make about ourselves, and ultimately, our actions. The good news, however, is that we can tackle these negative core beliefs, challenge them, and draw upon our strengths to smash the destructive negative core beliefs and develop new beliefs about ourselves. Table 4.8: New Core Beliefs provides a framework in which to practice developing new core beliefs. Please see the example below, and then work with the child on the blank forms in the Appendix and online to help them develop new core beliefs.

Chapter 4

Table 4.6: IMPACT OF CORE BELIEFS

Name: _____   Date: _____

Core belief	Assumption	Things I do/don't do because of core belief
I am not very good at talking with a group of people in social situations.	IF I am not good at talking with a group of people in social situations, THEN I will never make friends.	I have anxiety about interacting with a group of people in social situations, so I avoid parties and other social settings as much as I can.
I am good at running.	IF I am good at running, I might do okay in a sport where I have to run.	I joined the track team.

Table 4.7: FIND MY STRENGTHS TO CHALLENGE ASSUMPTIONS

Name: _____   Date: _____

Core belief	Assumption	Challenging the assumption and finding my strengths
I am not very good at talking with a group of people in social situations.	IF I'm not good at talking with a group of people in social situations, THEN I will never make friends.	I am good at one-to-one interactions, so I can start a conversation with one other person in the room instead of talking to a group of people.

Table 4.8: NEW CORE BELIEFS

Name: _____   Date: _____

Core belief	New core belief
I am not very good at talking with a group of people in social situations.	I am good at one-to-one conversations.
I am a horrible artist.	I draw fine for what I need to do at school.

EMOTION REGULATION

The above tables and figures helped you begin to sort through feelings, triggers, core beliefs, and assumptions with children and adolescents. The journey toward fully understanding feelings, triggers, core beliefs, and assumptions is lifelong. These exercises take children and adolescents one step closer to recognizing the factors that play a role in emotion regulation.

EVALUATE FIGHT-FLIGHT-FREEZE-FALL ASLEEP RESPONSE AND LIZARD THINKING

The Mind-Behavior Connection: An Examination of the Relationship Between Our Thoughts, Feelings, and Fight-Flight-Freeze-Fall Asleep Responses

Teaching children to focus on signature strengths and shift toward building resilience will assist them with establishing healthier thought patterns. In other words, if they can rid themselves of negative thoughts, their ability to manage our emotions increases.

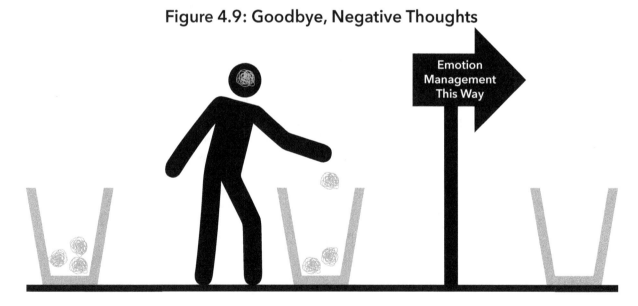

Figure 4.9: Goodbye, Negative Thoughts

Fight-Flight-Freeze-Fall Asleep Response and Lizard Thinking

Figure 4.9: Goodbye, Negative Thoughts makes emotion regulation look easy, but in reality, as we have witnessed throughout this book, it is far from an easy process. It is important to recognize every step a child takes toward effective emotion regulation, no matter how small the step might be. In the 1950s, Dr. Paul D. MacLean, a leading brain scientist of the twentieth century (Newman and Harris 2009), posited the brain was not just one entity, but three. As pictured in figure 4.10: The Three Entities of the Brain, he described the triune brain as including the limbic brain, which houses our emotions, the neocortex, which houses our higher-order thinking, and our brain stem, or reptilian brain, which is our survival brain. The interplay between our limbic brain and our reptilian brain is often the source of anxious responses.

Figure 4.10: The Three Entities of the Brain

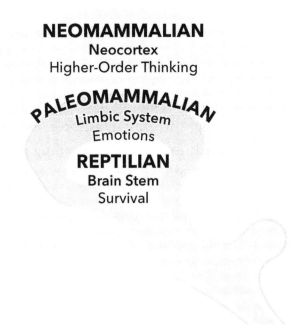

Our natural instinct is to survive. Although survival might not mean an actual fight, it does mean our adrenaline surges and our system prepares for a "fight." Lizard or reptilian brain thinking includes our raw, unprocessed response to a threat. Lizard responses lack cognitive processing (Barry 2006). For example, Matt tripped over a stick on the path while running. He reacted with his lizard brain and yelled at his mom for failing to warn him there was a stick in his way.

As discussed earlier, the opposite of lizard thinking is *wizard thinking*, which includes conscious problem-solving and constructive thinking (Barry 2006). Thinking like a wizard includes problem-solving and thinking before reacting. This ultimately leads to better emotion management. For example, if Matt used his wizard brain, he might have realized his mom could not see the stick. Instead of yelling at her, he might have asked his mom for a hug after he fell.

EMOTION REGULATION

Our survival instinct began in the days of cave people and continues today. However, our worries today are certainly different from those of our prehistoric ancestors—we typically are not running from large animals, actively engaging in fights, or hunting and gathering our food. There are, however, modern-day threats that trigger our survival instincts. These threats include national and local threats as well as threats we might experience in our daily lives. Living through a global pandemic certainly triggered our survival instincts. Children and adolescents may also experience a number of threats, including the pressure to succeed, bullying, negative online interactions, and exposure to violence, to name a few.

Our fight-flight-freeze-fall asleep instincts are critical in our daily lives and help to ensure our safety. Imagine for a moment that you are walking down the street and a woman is heading toward you on her bicycle. As she approaches, she suddenly swerves toward you. Your natural instinct is to jump out of the way to avoid a collision. This is an example of a fight-flight-freeze-fall asleep response, and in many cases, it comes in handy. However, there are times when our fight-flight-freeze-fall asleep response is not helpful. Imagine you fall down and feel embarrassed. Your friend is standing next to you. Your fight-flight-freeze-fall asleep response is to yell at your friend to go away. This response could hurt your friendship.

Talk about the above examples with the child in order to help them understand instinctual responses. Or pick a fight-flight-freeze-fall asleep situation from the child's life. (Or yours if the child is unable to think of an example.) Then talk through the questions below together in order to determine whether the child's instinctual response was effective in that situation:

1. Were you able to take a step back after the instinctual fight-flight-freeze-fall asleep response to accurately and adequately assess whether or not the situation was in fact threatening?

2. After the trigger, did the intensity and severity of your anxious reaction decrease?

If the situation was not a threat but the child reacted as if it was, then the child's natural instincts may be causing trouble for them. Similarly, if the intensity of the anxious reaction lingered, the child's fight-flight-freeze-fall asleep instincts warrant further investigation and intervention.

Chapter 4

BUMP!

Explore figure 4.11 with the child:

Imagine, for example, that a person bumped into you from behind by accident. What would happen with your fight-flight-freeze-fall asleep instincts if you perceived this bump as an intentional threat? How would your reptilian or lizard brain react?

Figure 4.11: BUMP!

| Person bumps you from behind. | I'M BEING ATTACKED! | Turn around and hit the person. |

Now help the child look at the difference in what might happen if they were mindful, examined all aspects of the surroundings, and responded accordingly, like a wizard.

| Person bumps you from behind. | I'M BEING ATTACKED! | Oh, Lizard, I'm not being attacked. This guy is running late to his flight and bumped me by accident. | Step to the side and let the man pass. |

Negative thoughts and perceptions are like a glorious meal for a lizard brain. They give it the fuel it needs, which causes anxiety and fear. However, we can teach children to be the boss of their lizard brain by taking charge of their thinking, examining their perceptions, and acting accordingly. Children can act like wizards and think positive, helpful thoughts instead of negative thoughts (Barry 2006)!

Try This

The following activities will help the child or adolescent take another step toward effective emotion regulation:

Burst Your Worry Bubbles: Imagine you are blowing bubbles or actually blow bubbles with the child. Encourage the child to pretend each bubble is a worry that fuels lizard thinking. Then, POP! POP! POP! the worry bubbles together.

EMOTION REGULATION

Stomp! Out Lizard Thinking: Encourage the child to take all of their negative thoughts out of their head by writing them on pieces of paper. Put the pieces of paper on the floor. Stomp! on each negative thought with the child. As you stomp, you can both release negative energy. Then, encourage the child to tear up the papers and put them in the trash. This demonstrates how the child can be in charge of their negative thoughts and feelings. (And the stomping gives them sensory input as an added bonus!)

Thinking Pitfalls: The Most Common Cognitive Distortions

It is important to understand cognitive distortions in order to more effectively regulate emotions. Burns (1989) described the common cognitive distortions:

- **All-or-nothing thinking:** Seeing things as black or white versus using rainbow thinking (Collucci 2011; Kerstein 2013). "I am either going to see the new *Star Trek* or I'm not going to see a movie at all."

- **Overgeneralization:** A negative event becomes the barometer by which you judge life. "I got a D on my math test. I'm *never* going to get good grades in math."

- **Mental filter:** A single negative comment or piece of information blocks out anything positive. "I set up dinner for my mom. Everything else came out well, but I burned the broccoli, so the whole dinner was ruined. I am a failure in the kitchen."

- **Discounting the positive:** All positive experiences are rejected. Nothing you do is good enough. "I got a 97 on the test, but I should've gotten 100%. I'm very disappointed in myself."

- **Jumping to conclusions:** A blanket negative interpretation of an event. Two types of distorted thinking are part of jumping to conclusions: *mind reading* and *fortune-telling*. In both, you draw conclusions and predictions that either someone is reacting negatively to you (mind reading) or that something bad will happen (fortune-telling).

- **Magnification:** Negative qualities and challenges are magnified while strengths are ignored or diminished. "I'm an awful soccer player. I shouldn't even step foot on the field."

- **Emotional reasoning:** The assumption that negative feelings or thoughts are actually the reality of a situation. "I am terrified to take standardized testing, so it must be really awful to have to take it."

- **"Should" statements:** There are two types of "should" statements: Those we direct at ourselves and those that we direct toward others. "I should be able to handle all of this homework." "Teachers shouldn't give this much homework." The "shoulds" we direct at ourselves can cause us to feel guilt and frustration. The "shoulds" we direct at others can cause anger, disappointment, and frustration (Burns 1989).

- **Labeling:** Attaching a negative label to yourself in an all-or-nothing thinking moment: "I'm stupid." Labeling can also occur in our interpretations of others' behaviors. "She's a mean person."

- **Personalization and blame:** Believing you are responsible for an incident in which you had limited or no control. Personalization and blame can also occur with others. We might believe someone caused a particular problem without examining our role in the situation. "My daughter is having a tantrum again. I must be a terrible parent," or, "Janie is chewing really loudly just to annoy me."

The concept of a thought distortion is quite complex and ambiguous. There are a number of ways to help children understand the concept of a thought distortion. You might try the following activities:

Tinted Glasses

For this activity, you will need sunglasses with tinted lenses. If you cannot find any, encourage the child to pretend the sunglasses you are using have tinted lenses. Hold up a piece of white paper. Ask the child, "What color is this paper?" Inevitably, the child will say, "White." Then put the glasses on and ask what color the child thinks the paper through the red lenses. Talk with the child about the ways the glasses distorted the color. You can describe the similarity between the glasses and the ways in which our thoughts become distorted.

Carnival Mirrors

Search for pictures on the internet that show the impact carnival mirrors have on our bodies. Explain that our thought patterns can be warped or distorted much like our bodies in carnival mirrors.

EMOTION REGULATION

Cellophane

You can use different-colored cellophane paper, much as you did with the tinted glasses in the activity above. Looking through green cellophane paper, for example, not only distorts the color but can also warp the item we are looking at. This distorted color or item represents the ways in which our thoughts become distorted.

Tricky Brain

It may be helpful to explain that our brain has ways of playing tricks on us and distorting our thoughts. Give examples of times you have noticed the child's brain playing tricks on them.

Evaluating Thought Patterns

Take a moment to help the child evaluate their thought patterns. You can use the diagram of the train below (figure 4.12) to help them identify thought distortions. By helping them develop a better understanding of their specific thought distortions, you can begin working toward new thought patterns that increase their ability to manage emotions.

Next, read the following directions to the child: "A thought distortion is listed on each of the train cars. Each thought distortion weighs the train down, preventing it from reaching its destination. Your job is to eliminate as many thought distortions as possible so that the train can reach its destination."

Then, look at each of the thought distortions. For each thought distortion, ask the child to answer the following question, "Do I think this way?" If the answer is no, then ask them to cross out the thought distortion and congratulate them. The child just lightened the train's load (and the anxiety they might possibly experience). If the answer is yes, then help them write a new, more positive and accurate thought under the thought distortion. This will lighten the train's load (and the child's anxiety), and the train can reach its destination. Please see figure 4.12: Distortion Train on the next page.

Figure 4.12: Distortion Train (page 1 of 6)

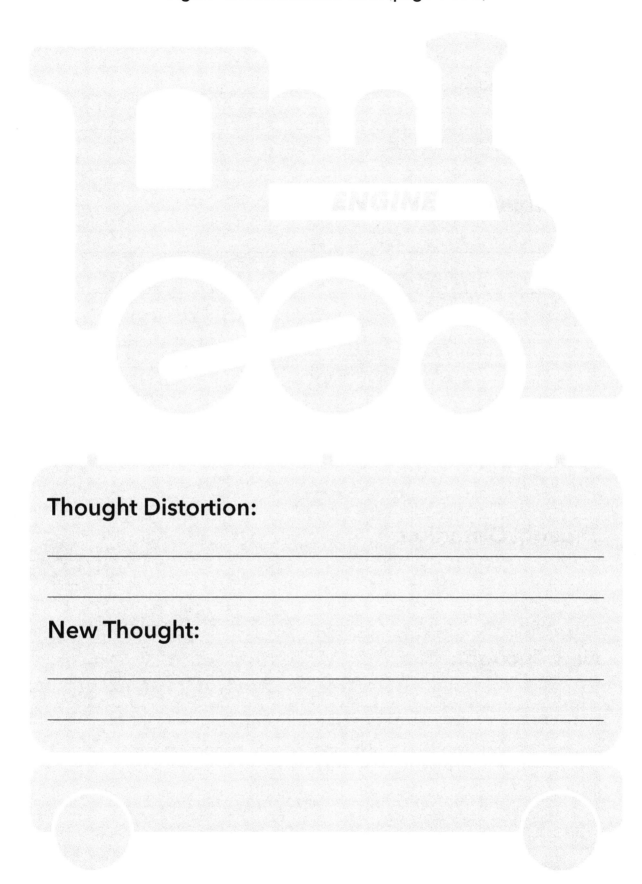

Thought Distortion:
_____
_____

New Thought:
_____
_____

Figure 4.12: Distortion Train (page 2 of 6)

Thought Distortion:
_____
_____

New Thought:
_____
_____

Thought Distortion:
_____
_____

New Thought:
_____
_____

Figure 4.12: Distortion Train (page 3 of 6)

Thought Distortion:
_____
_____

New Thought:
_____
_____

Thought Distortion:
_____
_____

New Thought:
_____
_____

Figure 4.12: Distortion Train (page 4 of 6)

Thought Distortion:
_____
_____

New Thought:
_____
_____

Thought Distortion:
_____
_____

New Thought:
_____
_____

Figure 4.12: Distortion Train (page 5 of 6)

Thought Distortion:
_____
_____

New Thought:
_____
_____

Thought Distortion:
_____
_____

New Thought:
_____
_____

Figure 4.12: Distortion Train (page 6 of 6)

Thought Distortion:
_____
_____

New Thought:
_____
_____

CABOOSE

Chapter 4

Flip It

As the saying goes, "Practice makes perfect." We are not striving for perfection. We are striving for growth and awareness. So, in our case, **practice makes growth**. Take some time to help the child or adolescent practice flipping thought distortions. Examples are listed below in figure 4.13: Flip It. The left cell represents one side of an index card. The right cell represents the other side of the index card. A blank version is located in the Appendix and online. You might even make index cards of the child's most common thought distortions so you can practice flipping those as well.

Figure 4.13: Flip It

EMOTION REGULATION

Radically Accepting Negative Thinking and Working to Find New Thoughts

Radical acceptance was first introduced by Linehan as an important step in emotion regulation. Radical acceptance allows us to recognize and accept the patterns we have and understand that the thought patterns emerged as a coping strategy of sorts. Radical acceptance is an important step in the direction of new, more adaptive thought patterns that will enable us to manage our emotions more effectively.

Help the child recognize that it is important not to beat themselves up over negative thoughts. At the same time, it is important not to invalidate thoughts. Negative thoughts are part of life. There are often perfectly good explanations for negative thinking. Life is challenging. Remember:

Figure 4.14: Beautiful Destinations

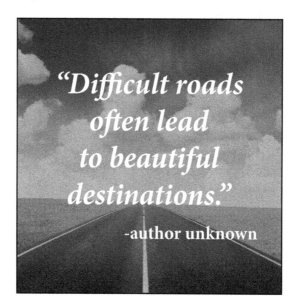

Help children understand the fact that negative thoughts and feelings have a way of piling up in the pretend cups we have inside our bodies that hold our stress, worries, sadness, and anxiety. In figure 4.15, the pitcher helps us operationalize the way stress can build up in our bodies. If we think of a pitcher as life and the water inside the pitcher as stress, we can imagine how much water might be in the pitcher each day. Life is stressful. Each time a stressful situation arises, a negative thought pops into our head, or we think in a distorted way, our cup fills up. If it fills too far and we forget to use strategies, our cups overflow, as illustrated in figure 4.16.

Chapter 4

Figure 4.15: Stress

Figure 4.16: Overflowing

Help the child understand that instead of piling negative thoughts ("I shouldn't be thinking this way") upon negative thoughts ("I'm so stupid. I always see the worst in everything") upon more negative thoughts ("I have no control over my lizard brain"), they can **accept** the fact that their lizard brain likes to take charge, and then work to be stronger than their lizard!

Also remind the child that the more negative thoughts they feed their lizard, the bigger it becomes, as pictured in figure 4.17.

However, the more strategies they use and the more times they flip their negative thinking, the smaller, quieter, and less annoying the lizard becomes. Little lizards, like the one in figure 4.18, are best!

Figure 4.17: Big Lizard

Figure 4.18: Little Lizard

EMOTION REGULATION

Take a moment to help the child write out the negative thoughts that fuel their lizard brain. Help the child think of a reason that justifies each of these thoughts. Then help them think of a new thought that might work better for them. Remind the child that understanding their thinking helps shrink the lizard! You may reference the examples shown in table 4.9 and then fill out the blank form that can be found in the appendix.

Table 4.9: SHRINK THE LIZARD THOUGHTS

Name: _____   Date: _____

Distorted Thought	This Is a Reasonable Thought Because ...	This New Thought Will Help Me Manage My Emotions
"I always freak out when I have to get a shot at the doctor's office."	There have been many times when I have gotten scared because shots hurt.	"I may have freaked out in the past, but I know I can be in charge of my feelings this time and stay calm. I know it will only hurt for a second."
"I will never run fast enough in the mile run at school today."	I have never finished first in the mile run before.	"I don't need to finish first or run faster than other people. Running the mile (or even walking the mile) is a great accomplishment.

A Note about Positive Thoughts

In addition to identifying and evaluating distorted thinking, it is also important to focus on what is going well with the child or adolescent's thinking. What positive thoughts are they having? What triggers positive moments or positive thoughts? How can the child increase the positive moments and thoughts they are having?

Take a moment to help the child evaluate their positive thoughts and emotions based on the examples in table 4.10.

Chapter 4

Table 4.10: EVALUATE YOUR THINKING

Name: _____   Date: _____

Positive Thought	This Thought Was Triggered By ...	These Positive Thoughts Helped Me Feel ...	Take Action
"Today is going to be great!"	Knowing I was going to get to eat at my favorite restaurant.	Excited Hopeful Happy	I am going to think about things I enjoy and add something each day to which I can look forward—like drinking my favorite drink or reading my favorite book.
"I am going to stay in control of my feelings today."	Knowing I am going to go to OT to help my body.	Happy Relieved Calm	I am going to try some of the strategies from OT on other days of the week to help me stay in control of my body.

ASSESS THE INTENSITY OF EMOTIONS

The intensity of our emotions can vary depending upon the trigger that sparked the emotion. This is true for positive as well as negative emotions. For example, if one of my daughters falls but does not get very hurt, I feel a small amount of sadness and worry. I also feel a large amount of relief (positive emotion). On the other hand, if one of them gets hurt badly, I feel a tremendous amount of sadness, grief, and worry. I might not experience any positive emotions at first because the intensity of my negative emotions is so high.

It is important to help children assess the intensity of their emotions and select tools that address the level of intensity they feel. It is also helpful to explain the fact that the intensity of emotions impacts the ability to make decisions, as illustrated on the next page in figure 4.19.

EMOTION REGULATION

Figure 4.19: Emotion intensity and decision-making from *My Sensory Book* by Lauren H. Kerstein, LCSW

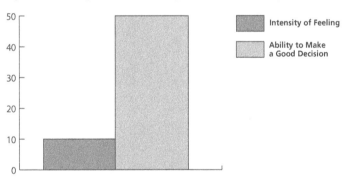

It is critical, then, to ensure the child's toolbox is filled with strategies that address each level of intensity. You might take a moment to look through table 4.11 with the child to assess the intensity of their emotions, the situation that caused them, and the strategies that might help.

Chapter 4

Table 4.11: EMOTION INTENSITY

Feeling	Intensity	Situations	Strategies
Angry	HIGH		
	MEDIUM		
	LOW		
Sad	HIGH		
	MEDIUM		
	LOW		
Nervous	HIGH		
	MEDIUM		
	LOW		

EMOTION REGULATION

Note: The concept of using shading to illustrate the intensity of feelings in this model is adapted from Jaffe and Gardner, *My Book Full of Feelings: How to Control and React to the Size of Your Emotions* (2006).

Feeling	Intensity	Situations	Strategies
Scared	HIGH		
	MEDIUM		
	LOW		
Happy	HIGH		
	MEDIUM		
	LOW		
Calm	HIGH		
	MEDIUM		
	LOW		

Chapter 4

It is helpful to establish a common language for describing emotion intensity. For example, you and the child can refer to the floors of an elevator to describe intensity, as shown in figure 4.20. The lower the floor, the lower the intensity; the higher the floor, the higher the intensity.

Figure 4.20: Elevator feelings

There have probably been times when you have seen an adolescent become red-hot angry. During these moments, a well-meaning person may have told the adolescent to take a deep breath. Unfortunately, taking one deep breath when red-hot angry probably won't help the adolescent enough. The adolescent may need a bigger strategy, one that will knock some of that anger out of their system. A bigger strategy might include taking a walk while listening to their favorite music, taking a bath, reading a great book, or talking to a friend.

Talk with your adolescent about what strategies help the most when they are red-hot angry. If they are not sure, it might be helpful to identify a few strategies and experiment with them to see if they help. Remember, repetition is one of the most important keys to learning (Frey and Fisher 2010). Often, we must repeat strategies for weeks at a time in order to foster change. Although the thought of trying something many times and even for weeks might seem overwhelming, remind the adolescent that the changes they are making will help them for the rest of their life, so it is well worth it.

EMOTION REGULATION

DIRECT THOUGHTS AND EMOTIONS TO A PLACE THAT IS MORE MANAGEABLE

The activities described here not only offer an opportunity to help the child recognize, evaluate, and assess their thoughts, feelings, and reactions but also to become the conductor and *direct* their own emotional orchestra, as pictured in figure 4.21. Each time the child's distorted thoughts creep in or the lizard tries to take charge, the child has the power to recognize the thoughts, evaluate fight-flight-freeze-fall asleep reactions, and assess the intensity of their emotions. All of this self-awareness and knowledge provides children with the tools they need in order to direct their thoughts and emotions to a place that is more manageable.

Figure 4.21: Conduct your emotional orchestra.

As you work with the child, keep in mind that part of directing thoughts and emotions is ensuring the child gets enough sleep, eats healthy foods, addresses physical illness, and exercises. All of these activities increase children's emotional strength by decreasing their vulnerability to emotions (Linehan 1993). Adding activities that give children pleasure and help them feel confident and competent also increases emotional strength.

Similarly, educate the child about the importance of avoiding things that can be harmful to them, such as drinking, drugs, endless hours on technology (feeding a technology addiction), and engaging in destructive activities such as picking fights or alienating those who care.

Take a moment to talk through table 4.12 with the child in order to help them increase the activities that support and enhance their emotional strength while decreasing activities that make them more vulnerable to emotional meltdowns.

Chapter 4

Table 4.12: EMOTIONAL STRENGTH

Name: _____   Date: _____

Things That Increase My Emotional Strength	Things That Make Me Vulnerable to Emotional Meltdowns
Reading a book for pleasure.	Spending time on Facebook.
Taking a walk.	Watching the news too close to bedtime.

Note: Stepping into the director's chair is not an easy process. Sometimes the child may feel like it is an uphill battle as they fight the chemicals in their brain, their self-image, their lizard/distorted thinking, and the intensity of their feelings. Remind the child that they have people in their life who care deeply and want to support them. Perhaps the child can let those who care for them walk beside them up the emotion regulation mountain to help them when they get stuck or fall down. The child might need to find "walking sticks," such as meditations, activities they enjoy, and positive thoughts in which they believe. These "walking sticks" will help the child avoid rocks and other obstacles. If the child can learn to believe in themselves, then they will begin to recognize that although managing emotions is a lifelong journey, it is a journey that will help them enjoy life a lot more. Figure 4.22 may help you as you talk about this with the child.

Figure 4.22: Climbing the emotion mountain

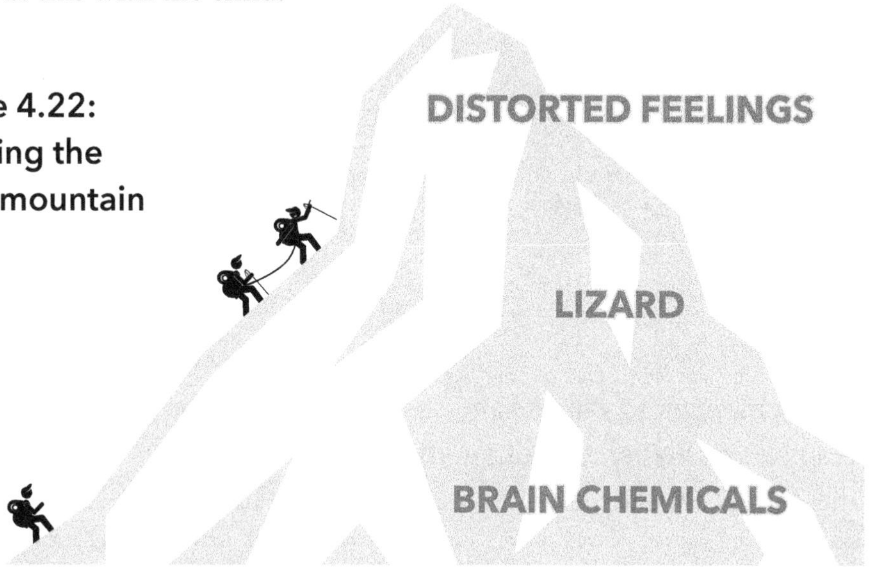

DISTORTED FEELINGS

LIZARD

BRAIN CHEMICALS

EMOTION REGULATION

**YOUR CHILD IS STRONGER THAN THEIR FEELINGS.
THEY CAN BE IN CHARGE OF THEIR FEELINGS AND EMOTIONS.**

Remind the child that they are stronger than their feelings. They can be in charge of their feelings and emotions. They have the power to take charge of their lizard thinking and increase their wizard thoughts (positive, adaptive thoughts).

Wizard Hat

Talk with the child about times they took charge of their feelings this past week. You can talk about it and/or write them in the wizard hat pictured in figure 4.23. The full-sized version is on page 140.

Figure 4.23: Think like a wizard.

The DBT Train

Take a moment to validate and support the work the child or adolescent has done around emotion regulation by talking through the DBT train pictured in figure 4.24. This train illustrates the many skills on which the child has worked and will continue to work in the years to come.

Figure 4.24: The DBT Train (page 1 of 2)

I CAN LEARN TO MANAGE MY EMOTIONS!

SKILLS

- I can learn to be mindful.
- I can learn to interact with others effectively.
- I can learn skills to manage my emotions.
- I can learn how to handle distress.

Figure 4.24: The DBT Train (page 2 of 2)

VALIDATION

- It's okay that there are things that trigger me.
- It's okay to have positive and negative thoughts when I'm triggered.
- It's okay to sit with those thoughts and also recognize there are other thoughts I can think that might help me feel better.
- It's okay to recognize that negative thoughts could lead to harmful actions.
- It's okay to recognize the harmful actions used to be my way to cope.
- It's okay to choose other actions that aren't hurtful.

RADICAL ACCEPTANCE

- I will accept the fact that I have thoughts in my head that are uncomfortable.
- I will not judge myself.
- I will not judge my thoughts.
- I will not judge my emotions.
- I will be in control of my emotions even when I have uncomfortable thoughts.
- I will treat myself fairly and with compassion.

SUMMARY

This chapter offered intervention strategies rooted in CBT, DBT and/or positive psychology that you can use with children, or children can use independently in order to manage their emotions more effectively. The more interventions you add to children's toolbox, the more successful they will be.

CHAPTER 5

CREATING AN EMOTION REGULATION PLAN FOR THE CHILD: THE REALITY OF EMOTION REGULATION

You have made it through the book. CONGRATULATIONS! You've helped the child or adolescent gather a lot of information and explore ways to regulate their emotions more effectively. Please read the following together and help them fill in the blanks below. This will help the child solidify the gains they have made, practice applying the information to real life, and increase confidence in the ability to take charge of their emotions.

- There will be triggers in your life.

- You will have feelings as a result of these triggers.

- Some of the triggers and feelings will be positive.

- Some of the triggers will be negative.

BUT...

You have an IDEA about how to manage your emotions:

- **Identify** triggers, feelings, and intensity.

- **Design** emotion regulation strategies.

- **Educate** yourself about the specific situations in which the strategies might be most helpful. Rehearse strategies with someone you trust to ensure you know how to carry them out effectively.

EMOTION REGULATION

- **Actively** use intervention strategies to increase your emotion regulation and decrease the intensity of your emotions. Reward yourself with praise, with a favorite activity, or by recording your success in a log when you use strategies.

You have the skills to **READ Yourself to be READY** to face these challenges.

- You can **RECOGNIZE** your triggers and beliefs.

- You can **EVALUATE** your fight-flight-freeze-fall asleep response and lizard thinking.

- You can **ASSESS** the intensity of your emotions.

- You can **DIRECT** your thoughts and emotions to a place that is more manageable.

- **YOU** are stronger than your feelings. **YOU** can be in charge of your feelings and emotions.

You can do the five As:

1. You can **Avoid** as many negative triggers as possible.

2. You can **Add** more positive experiences to your life.

3. You can **Accept** your feelings.

4. You can **Alter** your perception of yourself and move your feelings to a place that is more manageable.

5. You can **Act** when your feelings overwhelm you rather than giving up.

Ask the child or adolescent the following questions in figure 5.1 to support this newfound self-awareness. This form is available in the appendix and online.

Chapter 5

Figure 5.1: What Have You Learned?

Name: _____ Date: _____

What have you learned about yourself while reading this book?

What do you plan to do with this knowledge?

What activities help you manage your emotions better?

What situations make it harder for you to manage your emotions?

EMOTION REGULATION

A NEW TOOLBOX OF STRATEGIES

Throughout the book, you and the child have learned that certain tools help them better manage emotions. Encourage the child to fill in the blank toolbox, which is available online, with strategies that will help them better manage their emotions. These tools will help you for years to come!

Figure 5.2: My Toolbox

REFERENCES

Abramson, L. Y., Seligman, M. E. P., and Teasdale, J. D. (1978). "Learned Helplessness in Humans: Critique and Reformulation." *Journal of Abnormal Psychology*, 87(1), 49–74.

Adler Graduate School. (2014). "Alfred Adler: Theory and Application." Retrieved from http://www.alfredadler.edu/about/theory.

Akin-Little, K. A., Little, S. G., and Delligatti, N. (2004). "A Preventative Model of School Consultation: Incorporating Perspectives from Positive Psychology." *Psychology in the Schools*, 41(1), 155–162.

Allen, K. (2011). "Introduction to the Special Issue: Cognitive-Behavioral Therapy in the School Setting – Expanding the School Psychologist's Toolkit." *Psychology in the Schools*, 48(3), 215–222.

American Psychiatric Association. (2013). *Diagnostic and Statistical Manual of Mental Disorders* (5th ed.). Arlington, VA: Author.

Aspy, R., and Grossman, B.G. (2011). *The Ziggurat Model: A Framework for Designing Comprehensive Interventions for Individuals with High-Functioning Autism and Asperger Syndrome*. Shawnee Mission, KS: AAPC Publishing.

Attwood, T. (2003). "Frameworks for Behavioral Interventions." *Child and Adolescent Psychiatric Clinics of North America*, 12, 65–86.

Attwood, T., and Garnett, M. (2013). *CBT to Help Young People with Asperger's Syndrome (Autism Spectrum Disorder) to Understand and Express Affection*. London, UK: Jessica Kingsley Publishers.

Ayres, A. J. (2005). *Sensory Integration and the Child*. Los Angeles, CA: Western Psychological Services.

Barnhill, G. P., and Myles, B. S. (2001). "Attributional Style and Depression in Adolescents with Asperger Syndrome." *Journal of Positive Behavior Interventions*, 3(3), 175–182.

Barry, P. G. (2006). *How to be Brainwise: The Proven Method for Making Smart Choices*. Denver, CO: Innisfree Press.

Bass, C., van Nevel, J., and Swart, J. (2014). "A Comparison Between Dialectical Behavior Therapy, Mode Deactivation Therapy, Cognitive Behavioral Therapy, and Acceptance and Commitment Therapy in the Treatment of Adolescents." *International Journal of Behavioral Consultation and Therapy*, 9(2), 4–8.

Bearman, S. K., and Weisz, J. R. (2012). "Cognitive-Behavior Therapy." In E. Szigethy, J. R. Weisz, and R. L. Findling (Eds.), *Cognitive-Behavior Therapy for Children and Adolescents* (pp. 1–28). Washington, DC: American Psychiatric Publishing.

Beck, A. T., Wenzel, A., Riskind, J. H., Brown, G., and Steer, R. A. (2006). "Specificity of Hopelessness About Resolving Life Problems: Another Test of the Cognitive Model of Depression." *Cognitive Therapy Research*, 30, 773–781.

Bell, M. A., and Deater-Deckard, K. (2007). "Biological Systems and the Development of Self-Regulation: Integrating Behavior, Genetics, and Psychophysiology." *Journal of Development and Behavioral Pediatrics*, 28(5), 409–420.

Bellini, S. *Building Social Relationships 2: A Systematic Approach to Teaching Social Interaction Skills to Children and Adolescents on the Autism Spectrum*. Shawnee Mission, KS: AAPC Publishing (2006).

Bellini, S. "The Development of Social Anxiety in Adolescents with Autism Spectrum Disorders." *Focus on Autism and Other Developmental Disabilities* 21, no. 3 (2006): 138–145.

Bitsika, V., C. F. Sharpley, and R. Bell. "The Buffering Effect of Resilience upon Stress, Anxiety and Depression in Parents of a Child with an Autism Spectrum Disorder." *Journal of Developmental and Physical Disabilities* 25 (2013): 533–543.

Bowen, C. "Information for Families: Semantic and Pragmatic Difficulties." 2011. http://www.speech-language-therapy.com/.

Bridges, L. J., and W. S. Grolnick. "The Development of Emotional Self-Regulation in Infancy and Early Childhood." In *Social Development*, edited by N. Eisenberg, 185–211. Thousand Oaks, CA: Sage, 1995.

Briers, S. *Brilliant Cognitive Behavioral Therapy*. London, UK: Pearson Education, 2009.

Burns, D. D. *The Feeling Good Handbook*. New York: Penguin Books, 1989.

Chahar Mahali et al. "Associations of Negative Cognitions, Emotional Regulation, and Depression Symptoms across Four Continents: International Support for the Cognitive Model of Depression." *BMC Psychiatry* 20, no. 1 (2020): 1-12.

Chalfont, A. M., R. Rapee, and L. Carroll. "Treating Anxiety Disorders in Children with High Functioning Autism Spectrum Disorders: A Controlled Trial." *Journal of Autism and Developmental Disorders* 37 (2007): 1842–1857.

Chansky, T. E. *Freeing the Child from Negative Thinking*. Cambridge, MA: Da Capo Press, 2008.

Chansky, T. E. *Freeing the Child from Anxiety*, 2nd ed. New York: Harmony Books, 2014.

References

Collucci, A. *Big Picture Thinking: Using Central Coherence Theory to Support Social Skills*. Shawnee Mission, KS: AAPC Publishing, 2011.

Cotugno, A. J. "Social Competence and Social Skills Training and Intervention for Children with Autism Spectrum Disorder." *Journal of Autism and Developmental Disorders* 39 (2009): 1268–1277.

Craig, A. D. "How Do You Feel? Interoception: The Sense of the Physiological Condition of the Body." *Nature Reviews Neuroscience* 3, no. 8 (2002): 655-666.

Dawson, P., and R. Guare. *Executive Skills in Children and Adolescents: A Practical Guide to Assessment and Intervention*. New York: The Guilford Press, 2004.

Dawson, P., and R. Guare. *Smart but Scattered*. New York: Guilford Press, 2009.

DeAngelis, T. "Anxiety among kids is on the rise. Wider access to CBT may provide needed solutions." *American Psychological Association* 53, no. 7 (2022): 38.

Decety, J., and P. L. Jackson. "A Social-Neuroscience Perspective on Empathy." *Current Directions in Psychological Science* 15, no. 2 (2006): 54-58.

de Vries, M., and H. M. Geurts. "Cognitive Flexibility in ASD; Task Switching with Emotional Faces." *Journal of Autism and Developmental Disorders* 42 (2012): 2558–2568.

Denham, S. A., H. H. Bassett, E. Way, M. Mincic, K. Zinsser, and K. Graling. "Preschoolers' Emotion Knowledge: Self-Regulatory Foundations, and Predictions of Early School Success." *Cognition and Emotion* 26, no. 4 (2012): 667–679.

Ekas, N. V., D. M. Lickenbrock, and J. M. Braungart-Rieker. "Developmental Trajectories of Emotion Regulation across Infancy: Do Age and the Social Partner Influence Temporal Patterns?" *Infancy* 18, no. 5 (2013): 729–754.

Engle, E., S. Gadischkie, N. Roy, and D. Nunziato. "Dialectical Behavior Therapy for a College Population: Applications at Sarah Lawrence College and Beyond." *Journal of College Student Psychotherapy* 27 (2013): 11–30.

Feigenbaum, J. "Dialectical Behaviour Therapy: An Increasing Evidence Base." *Journal of Mental Health* 16, no. 1 (2007): 51–68.

Fisak, B. J., D. Richard, and A. Mann. "The Prevention of Child and Adolescent Anxiety: A Meta-analytic Review." *Prevention Science* 12 (2011): 255–268.

Flavell, J. H. "Cognitive Development: Children's Knowledge about the Mind." *Annual Review of Psychology* 50 (1999): 21–45.

EMOTION REGULATION

Frey, N., and D. Fisher. "Reading and the Brain: What Early Childhood Educators Need to Know." *Early Childhood Education* 38 (2010): 103–110.

Fried, L. "Teaching Teachers about Emotion Regulation in the Classroom." *Australian Journal of Teacher Education* 36, no. 3 (2011): 1–10.

Frith, U., and F. Happé. "Autism: Beyond 'Theory of Mind.'" *Cognition* 50 (1994): 115–132.

Geller, L. "Emotional Regulation and Autism Spectrum Disorder." *Autism Spectrum Quarterly*, Summer (2005): 14–17.

Goleman, D. *Emotional Intelligence*. New York: Bantam Books, 1995.

Groden, J., A. Kantor, C. R. Woodard, and L. P. Lipsitt. *How Everyone on the Autism Spectrum, Young and Old, Can Become Resilient, Be More Optimistic, Enjoy Humor, Be Kind, and Increase Self-efficacy: A Positive Psychology Approach*. London: Jessica Kingsley Publishers, 2011.

Gross, J. J., and O. P. John. "Individual Differences in Two Emotion Regulation Processes: Implications for Affect, Relationships, and Well-being." *Journal of Personality and Social Psychology* 85 (2003): 348–362.

Groves, S., H. S. Backer, W. van den Bosch, and A. Miller. "Review: Dialectical Behaviour Therapy with Adolescents." *Child and Adolescent Mental Health* 17, no. 2 (2012): 65–75.

Hadjiosif, M. "Theoretical Paper: From Strategy to Process: Validation in Dialectical Behaviour Therapy." *Counselling Psychology Review* 28, no. 1 (2013): 72–80.

Happé, F., and U. Frith. "The Weak Coherence Account: Detail-focused Cognitive Style in Autism Spectrum Disorders." *Journal of Autism and Developmental Disorders* 35, no. 1 (2006): 3–25.

Hartmann, K., M. Urbano, K. Manswer, and L. Okwara. "Modified Dialectical Behavior Therapy to Improve Emotion Regulation in Autism Spectrum Disorders." In *Autism Spectrum Disorders New Research*, edited by C. E. Richardson and R. A. Wood, 41–72. New York: Nova Science Publishers, 2012.

Harvey, P., and J. A. Penzo. *Parenting a Child Who Has Intense Emotions: Dialectical Behavior Therapy Skills to Help the Child Regulate Emotional Outbursts and Aggressive Behaviors*. Oakland, CA: New Harbinger Publications, 2009.

Henderson, N. *The Resiliency Workbook: Bounce Back Stronger, Smarter, and with Real Self-esteem*. Solvang, CA: Resiliency in Action, 2012.

Hesslinger, B., L. Tebartz van Elst, E. Nyberg, P. Dykierek, H. Richter, M. Berner, and D. Ebert. "Psychotherapy of Attention Deficit Hyperactivity Disorder in Adults a Pilot Study Using a Structured Skills Training Program." *European Archives of Psychiatry and Clinical Neuroscience* 252 (2002): 177–184.

References

Hirshfeld-Becker, D. R., R. Masek, A. Henin, L. R. Blakely, D. C. Rettew, L. Y. Dufton, ... J. Biderman. "Cognitive-behavioral Intervention with Young Anxious Children." *Harvard Review Psychiatry* 16 (2008): 113–125.

Hranov, L. G. "Comorbid Anxiety and Depression: Illumination of a Controversy." *International Journal of Psychiatry in Clinical Practice* 11, no. 3 (2007): 171-189.

Hutman, T., and M. Dapretto. "The Emergence of Empathy During Infancy." *Cognition*, Brain, Behavior. An Interdisciplinary Journal 13, no. 4 (2009): 367–390.

Igna, R., and S. Ştefan. "Comparing Cognitive Strategies in the Process of Emotion Regulation." *Journal of Evidence-Based Psychotherapies* 15, no. 2 (2015): 251–266.

Jennings, J. L., and J. A. Apsche. "The Evolution of a Fundamentally Mindfulness-Based Treatment Methodology: From DBT and ACT to MDT and Beyond." *International Journal of Behavioral Consultation and Therapy* 9, no. 2 (2014): 1–4.

Keehn, R.H.M., A.J. Lincoln, M.Z. Brown, and D.A. Chavira. "The Coping Cat Program for Children with Anxiety and Autism Spectrum Disorder: A Pilot Randomized Controlled Trial." *Journal of Autism and Developmental Disorders* 43 (2013): 57–67.

Kerns, C. M., and P. C. Kendall. "The Presentation and Classification of Anxiety in Autism Spectrum Disorder." *Clinician Psychology Science and Practice* 19, no. 4 (2013): 323–347.

Kerstein, L. H. *My Sensory Book: Working Together to Explore Sensory Issues and the Big Feelings They Can Cause: A Workbook for Parents, Professionals, and Children.* Shawnee Mission, KS: AAPC Publishing, 2008.

Kerstein, L. H. *A Week of Switching, Shifting, and Stretching: How to Make My Thinking More Flexible.* Shawnee Mission, KS: AAPC Publishing, 2013.

Kopp, C.B. "Antecedents of Self-Regulation: A Developmental Perspective." *Developmental Psychology* 18, no. 2 (1982): 199–214.

Kring, A. M., and D. M. Sloan, eds. *Emotional Regulation and Psychopathology.* New York: The Guilford Press, 2010.

Lenz, A. S., R. Taylor, M. Fleming, and N. Serman. "Effectiveness of Dialectical Behavior Therapy for Treating Eating Disorders." *Journal of Counseling and Development* 92 (2013): 26–35.

Leijten, P., M. A. J. Raaijmakers, B. Orobio de Castro, E. van den Ban, and W. Matthys. "Effectiveness of the Incredible Years Parenting Program for Families with Socioeconomically Disadvantaged and Ethnic Minority Backgrounds." *Journal of Clinical Child and Adolescent Psychology* 18 (2015): 1–15.

Linehan, M. M. *Skills Training Manual for Treating Borderline Personality Disorder*. New York: The Guilford Press, 1993.

Maack, D.J., E. Buchanan, and J. Young. "Development and Psychometric Investigation of an Inventory to Assess Fight, Flight, and Freeze Tendencies: The Fight, Flight, Freeze Questionnaire." *Cognitive Behavior Therapy* 44, no. 2 (2015): 117–127.

MacPherson, H. A., J. S. Cheavens, and M. A. Fristad. "Dialectical Behavior Therapy for Adolescents: Theory, Treatment Adaptations, and Empirical Outcomes." *Clinical Child and Family Psychology Review* 16 (2013): 59–80.

Mahler, K.J. Interoception: *The Eighth Sensory System: Practice Solutions for Improving Self-Regulation, Self-Awareness and Social Understanding of Individuals with Autism Spectrum and Related Disorders*. Shawnee Mission, KS: AAPC, 2015.

Marques, S. C., J. L. Pais-Ribeiro, and S. J. Lopez. "The Role of Positive Psychology Constructs in Predicting Mental Health and Academic Achievement in Children and Adolescents: A Two-Year Longitudinal Study." *Journal of Happiness Studies* 12 (2011): 1049–1062.

Matson, J. L., and L. W. Williams. "Depression and Mood Disorders Among Persons with Autism Spectrum Disorders." *Research in Developmental Disabilities* 35 (2014): 2003–2007.

Mathersul, D., S. McDonald, and J. A. Rushby. "Understanding Advanced Theory of Mind and Empathy in High-Functioning Adults with Autism Spectrum Disorder." *Journal of Clinical and Experimental Neuropsychology* 35, no. 6 (2013): 655–668.

Mazefsky, C. A., K. A. Pelphrey, and R. E. Dahl. "The Need for a Broader Approach to Emotion Regulation Research in Autism." *Child Development Perspectives* 6, no. 1 (2012): 92–97.

Mazefsky, C.A., and S.W. White. "Emotion Regulation: Concepts and Practice in Autism Spectrum Disorder." *Child and Adolescent Psychiatric Clinics of North America* 23, no. 1 (2014): 15–24.

McGilloway, S., G. N. Mhaille, T. Bywater, M. Furlong, Y. Leckey, P. Kelly, ... M. Donnelly. "A Parenting Intervention for Childhood Behavioral Problems: A Randomized Controlled Trial in Disadvantaged Community-Based Settings." *Journal of Consulting and Clinical Psychology* 80, no. 1 (2012): 116–127.

McKay, M., J. C. Wood, and J. Brantley. *The Dialectical Behavior Therapy Skills Workbook: Practicing DBT Exercises for Learning Mindfulness, Interpersonal Effectiveness, Emotion Regulation and Distress Tolerance*. Oakland, CA: New Harbinger Publications, 2007.

Monsell, S. "Task Switching." TRENDS in *Cognitive Sciences* 7, no. 3 (2003): 134–140.

Newman, J. D., and J. C. Harris. "The Scientific Contributions of Paul D. Maclean." *The Journal of Nervous and Mental Disease* 197, no. 1 (2009): 3–5.

References

O'Grady, P. *Positive Psychology in the Elementary School Classroom*. New York: W.W. Norton and Company, 2013.

Owens, R.L., and M.M. Patterson. "Positive Psychological Interventions for Children: A Comparison of Gratitude and Best Possible Selves Approaches." *The Journal of Genetic Psychology* 174, no. 4 (2013): 403–428.

Perepletchikova, F., S. R. Axelrod, J. Kaufman, B. J. Rounsaville, H. Douglas-Palumberi, and A. L. Miller. "Adapting Dialectical Behavior Therapy for Children: Towards a New Research Agenda for Paediatric Suicidal and Non-Suicidal Self-Injurious Behavior." *Child and Adolescent Mental Health* 16, no. 2 (2011): 116–121.

Peterson, C. *A Primer in Positive Psychology*. New York: Oxford University Press, 2006.

Peterson, C. "The Strengths Revolution: A Positive Psychology Perspective." *Reclaiming Children and Youth* 21, no. 4 (2013): 7–14.

Rapee, R. M. "The Preventative Effects of a Brief, Early Intervention for Preschool-Aged Children at Risk for Internalizing: Follow-up into Middle Adolescence." *The Journal of Child Psychology and Psychiatry* 54, no. 7 (2013): 780–788.

Rapee, R. M., A. Wignall, S. H. Spence, V. Cobham, and H. Lyneham. *Helping Your Anxious Child: A Step-by-Step Guide for Parents*. Oakland, CA: New Harbinger Publications, 2008.

Reaven, J. A. "Children with High-Functioning Autism Spectrum Disorders and Co-occurring Anxiety Symptoms: Implications for Assessment and Treatment." *Journal for Specialists in Pediatric Nursing* 14, no. 3 (2009): 192–199.

Reaven, J., A. Blakely-Smith, E. Leuthe, E. Moody, and S. Hepburn. "Facing Your Fears in Adolescence: Cognitive-Behavioral Therapy for High-Functioning Autism Spectrum Disorders and Anxiety." *Autism Research and Treatment* 2012 (2012): 1–13.

Rieffe, C., M. Camodeca, L. B. C. Pouw, A. M. C. Lange, and L. Stockmann. "Don't Anger Me! Bullying, Victimization, and Emotion Dysregulation in Young Adolescents with ASD." *European Journal of Developmental Psychology* 9, no. 3 (2012): 351–370.

Röll, J., U. Koglin, and F. Petermann. "Emotion Regulation and Childhood Aggression: Longitudinal Associations." *Child Psychiatry and Human Development* 43 (2012): 909–923.

Rueda, M. R., and M. K. Rothbart. "The Influence of Temperament on the Development of Coping: The Role of Maturation and Experience." In *Coping and the Development of Regulation*, edited by E. A. Skinner and M. J. Zimmer-Gembeck, 19–31

Salovey, P., and J. D. Mayer. "Emotional Intelligence." *Imagination, Cognition, and Personality* 9 (1990): 185–211.

Schipper, M., and F. Petermann. "Relating Empathy and Emotion Regulation: Do Deficits in Empathy Trigger Emotion Dysregulation?" *Social Neuroscience* 8, no. 1 (2013): 101–107.

Seligman, M. E. P. *Learned Optimism*. New York: Knopf, 1991.

Seligman, M. E. P., R. M. Ernst, J. Gillham, K. Reivich, and M. Linkins. "Positive Education: Positive Psychology and Classroom Interventions." *Oxford Review of Education* 35, no. 3 (2009): 293–311.

Shaker-Naeeni, H., T. Govender, and U. Chowdhury. "Cognitive Behavioural Therapy for Anxiety in Children and Adolescents with Autism Spectrum Disorder." *British Journal of Medical Practitioners* 7, no. 3 (2014): 7–15.

Silk, J. S., L. Steinberg, and A. S. Morris. "Adolescents' Emotion Regulation in Daily Life: Links to Depressive Symptoms and Problem Behavior." *Child Development* 74, no. 6 (2003): 1869–1880.

Sofronoff, K., T. Attwood, S. Hinton, and I. Levin. "A Randomized Controlled Trial of a Cognitive Behavioural Intervention for Anger Management in Children Diagnosed with Asperger's Syndrome." *Journal of Autism and Developmental Disorders* 37 (2007): 1203–1214.

Stallard, P. *Think Good—Feel Good: A Cognitive Behaviour Therapy Workbook for Children and Young People*. London, UK: John Wiley and Sons, Ltd., 2002.

Suveg, C., E. Sood, J.S. Comer, and P.C. Kendall. "Changes in Emotion Regulation Following Cognitive-Behavioral Therapy for Anxious Youth." *Journal of Clinical Child and Adolescent Psychology* 38, no. 3 (2009): 390–401.

Swales, M. A. "Dialectical Behaviour Therapy: Description, Research, and Future Directions." *International Journal of Behavioral Consultation and Therapy* 5, no. 2 (2009): 164–171.

Szigethy, E., J. R. Weisz, and R. L. Findling, eds. *Cognitive-Behavior Therapy for Children and Adolescents*. Washington, DC: American Psychiatric Publishing, 2012.

Upshaw, M. B., C.R. Kaiser, and J. A. Sommerville. "Parents' Empathic Perspective Taking and Altruistic Behavior Predicts Infants' Arousal to Others' Emotions." *Frontiers in Psychology* 6 (2015): 1–11.

Valentine, S. E., S. M. Bankoff, R. M. Poulin, E. B. Reidler, and D. W. Pantalone. "The Use of Dialectical Behavior Therapy Skills Training as Stand-Alone Treatment: A Systematic Review of the Treatment Outcome Literature." *Journal of Clinical Psychology* 71, no. 1 (2015): 1–20.

Velting, O. N., N. J. Setzer, and A. M. Albano. "Update on and Advances in Assessment and Cognitive-Behavioral Treatment of Anxiety Disorders in Children and Adolescents." *Professional Psychology: Research and Practice* 35, no. 1 (2004): 42–54.

References

Vermeulen, P. *Autism as Context Blindness*. Shawnee Mission, KS: AAPC Publishing, 2012.

Vohs, K.D., and R.F. Baumeister, eds. "Understanding Self-Regulation." In *Handbook of Self-Regulation: Research, Theory, and Applications*, 1–9. New York: The Guilford Press, 2004.

White, S.W., A. Albano, C. Johnson, C. Kasari, T. Ollendick, A. Klin, et al. "Development of a Cognitive-Behavioral Intervention Program to Treat Anxiety and Social Deficits in Teens with High-Functioning Autism." *Clinical Child and Family Psychotherapy Review* 13, no. 1 (2010): 77–90.

White, S. W., D. Oswald, T. Ollendick, and L. Scahill. "Anxiety in Children and Adolescents with Autism Spectrum Disorders." *Clinical Psychological Review* 29, no. 3 (2009): 216–229.

Wicks-Nelson, R., and A. C. Israel. *Abnormal Child and Adolescent Psychology*. Upper Saddle River, NJ: Pearson, 2009.

Wilkes-Gillan, S., A. Bundy, R. Cordier, and M. Lincoln. "Eighteen-Month Follow-Up of a Play-Based Intervention to Improve the Social Play Skills of Children with Attention Deficit Hyperactivity Disorder." *Australian Occupational Therapy Journal* 61 (2014): 299–307.

Williams, M. S., and S. Shellenberger. *How Does Your Engine Run? A Leader's Guide to the Alert Program for Self-Regulation*. Albuquerque, MN: TherapyWorks, 1996.

Wissing, M. P., and C. van Eeden. "Empirical Clarification of the Nature of Psychological Well-Being." *South African Journal of Psychology* 32, no. 1 (2002): 32–44.

Wood, J. J., A. Drahota, K. Sze, M. Van Dyke, K. Decker, C. Fujii, ... M. Spiker. "Brief Report: Effects of Cognitive Behavioral Therapy on Parent-Reported Autism Symptoms in School-Age Children with High-Functioning Autism." *Journal of Autism and Developmental Disorders* 39 (2009): 1608–1612.

Yeh, Z-T. "Role of Theory of Mind and Executive Function in Explaining Social Intelligence: A Structural Equation Modeling Approach." *Aging and Mental Health* 17, no. 5 (2013): 527–534.

Zager, D. "Positive Psychology and Autism Spectrum Disorders." In *The Oxford Handbook of Positive Psychology and Disability*, edited by M. L. Wehmeyer, 494–505. New York, NY, US: Oxford University Press, 2013.

RESOURCES

The following websites and references will help you on your journey toward more effective emotion regulation.

GENERAL EMOTION REGULATION RESOURCES

The Incredible Years: http://incredibleyears.com

Heroes/Leaders/Champions: http://heroesleaderschampions.org/

Kids Relaxation: http://kidsrelaxation.com/

Social Stories: http://carolgraysocialstories.com/

Gray, C. (1993). *The Original Social Story Book*. Arlington, TX: Future Horizons.

Gray, C. (1994). *Comic Strip Conversations*. Arlington, TX: Future Horizons.

Gray, C. (2000). *The New Social Story Book*. Arlington, TX: Future Horizons.

COGNITIVE BEHAVIORAL THERAPY RESOURCES

Websites

Attwood T. (n.d.) *Modifications to Cognitive Behaviour Therapy to Accommodate the Cognitive Profile*. Retrieved from http://www.tonyattwood.com.au/index.php/publications/by-tony-attwood/archived-papers/81-modifications-to-cognitive-behaviour-therapy-to-accommodate-the-cognitive-profile

Autism Teaching Strategies: http://autismteachingstrategies.com

The BrainWise Program: http://www.brainwise-plc.org/

Therapist aid: therapy worksheets, tools, and handouts for mental health counselors: http://www.therapistaid.com/therapy-worksheets/cbt/children

EMOTION REGULATION

Books

Barry, P. G. (2006). *How to Be Brainwise: The Proven Method for Making Smart Choices*. Denver, CO: Innisfree Press.

Kerstein, L. H. (2013). *A Week of Switching, Shifting, and Stretching: How to Make My Thinking More Flexible*. Shawnee Mission, KS: AAPC Publishing.

Stallard, P. (2002). *Think Good—Feel Good: A Cognitive Behaviour Therapy Workbook for Children and Young People*. London: John Wiley and Sons Ltd.

DIALECTICAL BEHAVIOR THERAPY RESOURCES

Websites

Calm for Kids: http://www.calmforkids.com (Christiane Kerr [who began Calm for Kids] also has wonderful meditations for children available for Apple products.)

Cognitive Behaviour Therapy Self-Help Resources. (n.d.). Dialectical behavior therapy. Retrieved from http://www.getselfhelp.co.uk/dbt.htm

HelpGuide.Org. (n.d.). Benefits of mindfulness. Retrieved from http://www.helpguide.org/harvard/benefits-of-mindfulness.htm

Mindful Hub: http://mindfulhub.com/

Mindful Life Program: https://mindfullifeprogram.org/

Mindful Life: http://mindfullifetoday.com/mindfulness-programs/.

The Plum Tree: http://www.theplumtree.net

Books

Henderson, N. (2012). *The Resiliency Workbook: Bounce Back Stronger, Smarter, and with Real Self-Esteem*. Solvang, CA: Resiliency in Action.

McKay, M., Wood, J. C., and Brantley, J. (2007). *The Dialectical Behavior Therapy Skills Workbook: Practicing DBT Exercises for Learning Mindfulness, Interpersonal Effectiveness, Emotion Regulation and Distress Tolerance*. Oakland, CA: New Harbinger Publications.

Resources

Perepletchikova, F., Axelrod, S. R., Kaufman, J., Rounsaville, B. J., Douglas-Palumberi, H., and Miller, A. L. (2011). "Adapting Dialectical Behavior Therapy for Children: Towards a New Research Agenda for Paediatric Suicidal and Non-Suicidal Self-Injurious Behavior." *Child and Adolescent Mental Health*, 16(2), 116–121. (This reference contains a very helpful list of experiential exercises in Appendix A.)

POSITIVE PSYCHOLOGY RESOURCES

Websites

Centre for Confidence: http://www.centreforconfidence.co.uk/pp/emilysnews.php

Positive Psychology Center: http://www.ppc.sas.upenn.edu

Safe and Caring Schools and Communities: http://resources.safeandcaring.ca/resource-safe/

University of Pennsylvania Authentic Happiness: http://www.authentichappiness.com

Books

Henderson, N. (2012). *The Resiliency Workbook: Bounce Back Stronger, Smarter, and with Real Self-Esteem*. Solvang, CA: Resiliency in Action.

O'Grady, P. (2013). *Positive Psychology in the Elementary School Classroom*. New York: W.W. Norton and Company.

A SAMPLE OF PICTURE BOOKS AND GRAPHIC NOVELS FOR EMOTION DECODING

Babay, M. (2021). *I'm a Gluten-Sniffing Service Dog*. Illinois: Albert Whitman & Co.

Bell, C. (2014). *El Deafo*. New York: Abrams.

Dubbin, L. (2024). *Perfect Match: The Story of Althea Gibson and Angela Buxton*. Minneapolis: Kar-Ben Publishing.

Frawley, K. (2024). *Lighthouse and the Little Boat*. New York: Quill Tree Books.

Kerstein, L.H. (2019). *Rosie the Dragon and Charlie Make Waves*. New York: Two Lions.

EMOTION REGULATION

Kerstein, L.H. (2020). *Rosie the Dragon and Charlie Say Good Night*. New York: Two Lions.

Kerstein, L.H. (2021). *Home for a While*. Wisconsin: Magination Press.

Kerstein, L.H. (2023). *Remembering Sundays with Grandpa*. Minnesota: Beaming Books.

Lim, H. (2024). *Sourgrass*. New York: Beach Lane Books.

Pastro, J. (2024). *Lucas and the Capoeira Circle*. New York: Atheneum Books for Young Readers.

Schulte, A.R. (2021). *Dancing with Daddy*. New York: Two Lions.

Schulz, B. (2020). *Don't Wake the Dragon*. New York: Clever Publishing.

Stiefel, C. (2019). *My Name is Wakawakaloch!* New York: Houghton Mifflin Harcourt.

Stocker, S. (2022). *Listen: How Evelyn Glennie, a Deaf Girl, Changed Percussion*. New York: Dial Books for Young Readers.

Thurman, B.J. (2024). *Forever and Always*. New York: HarperCollins Children's Books.

Williams, L. and Scheemann, K. (2020). *Go With The Flow*. New York: First Second.

Williams, L. and Scheemann, K. (2023). *Look on the Bright Side*. New York: First Second.

APPENDIX
ASSESSING AND SUPPORTING SKILLS

A BRIEF NOTE ABOUT ASSESSMENT MEASURES

Assessing a child's strengths and weaknesses is challenging. You may use anecdotal information based on your experiences as well as standardized measures. An exploration of standardized measures is not within the scope of this book. However, I would like to highlight two measures that may be helpful in designing targeted and individualized interventions: the Underlying Characteristics Checklist (UCC) and the Individual Strengths and Skills Inventory (ISSI) (Aspy and Grossman 2011). These instruments were developed by Ruth Aspy, PhD, and Barry Grossman, PhD, and provide questionnaires for both the child and the adult working with the child (Aspy and Grossman 2011). The UCC and ISSI both examine the following areas:

- Social
- Restricted patterns of behavior interests and activities
- Communication
- Sensory differences
- Cognitive differences
- Motor differences
- Emotional vulnerability

In addition, the UCC examines "known medical or other biological factors." These two measures may assist you as you assess children, especially because the UCCs are designed to adapt to many different situations.

If you would like more information regarding assessment, it might be helpful to consult with professionals who specialize in assessment. For example, there are psychologists and neuropsychologists who provide comprehensive testing in order to assess many aspects of a child. You might also seek the assistance of a clinician trained in a particular area of concern. For example, a speech-language pathologist can assist you with a further assessment of communication and pragmatic concerns, while an occupational therapist can help you

EMOTION REGULATION

assess sensory needs, including interoception. Finally, you can contact a multidisciplinary team to provide a team diagnostic assessment. A full assessment can often be a helpful component of effective interventions.

A SAMPLE OF AREAS THAT OFTEN REQUIRE SUPPORT

A number of factors, skills, and traits were described in chapter 2. These factors, skills, and traits facilitate more effective emotion regulation. You probably found that the child had strengths in some areas and challenges in others. The following intervention strategies may be useful in strengthening the skill areas in which children have relative challenges. The more you help children strengthen the factors, skills, and traits associated with emotion regulation, the more effectively they will manage their emotions.

Interoception

Interoception, the ability to perceive internal signals in your body and react accurately and appropriately to these signals is an important skill to consider as you assist the child with increased emotion regulation. The ability to recognize the body's signals (i.e., an upset stomach), perceive the associated emotion, develop an appropriate action plan, and carry out this plan facilitates more effective emotion regulation.

Mindfulness and meditation have received attention in the literature as strategies that can increase interoceptive awareness (IA) (Mahler 2015). Strategies such as a body chart, which draws a child's attention to body parts and corresponding sensations, can be quite helpful (Mahler 2015).

For more information and strategies, please refer to Ms. Mahler's book *Interoception: The Eighth Sensory System: Practical Solutions for Improving Self-Regulation, Self-Awareness and Social Understanding of Individuals with Autism Spectrum and Related Disorders*.

Motor Skills

As we discussed, any areas of challenge can create anxiety for children. If children struggle with motor skills, they may be anxious that they will not be able to "keep up" with sports, physical education classes, and other activities that require motor skills. First, remind children of the things they do well. Then, assist children with identifying possible avenues for additional support. This may include an occupational therapist or physical therapist. The stronger children's motor skills, the more effectively they can access the strategies they need for emotion regulation.

Appendix

Theory of Mind

The first step in strengthening ToM is to increase children's understanding of this concept. The following scenario will help you explore ToM with children.

A child is reading her favorite book, and her mom comes home with groceries. If the child uses her ToM skills and tries to understand the different thoughts, feelings, and perspectives her mom might be having, she might think which of the following statements? (Circle all that apply):

1. My mom probably needs help carrying the groceries inside.

2. My mom feels tired from grocery shopping. She wants help.

3. My mom will just bring in all of the groceries and does not care if anyone helps her.

4. My mom likes it when I ignore her when she needs help.

5. My mom might have driven home hoping someone would be home to help her when she arrived.

It is important to help children understand the fact that the ability to recognize that others might experience an event or situation in their own unique way can increase positive social interactions. In addition, the more we understand emotions in others and ourselves, the more effectively we might manage these emotions.

The following scenario involving the man and the dog might assist the child with developing an understanding of the components of ToM and the ability to utilize many relationship skills simultaneously in order to better understand a situation.

In order to help the child make sense of this social scenario and identify the thoughts and feelings involved, look at the following with the child:

- The contextual clues (What is the dog doing? What is happening around the man and the dog?)

EMOTION REGULATION

- The man's nonverbals (including the feeling on their face and their arms crossed over their chest)

- The intensity of emotion reflected in the man's body

With that information in mind, you can begin to help the child flexibly think about answers to the following questions:

- What thoughts are in this man's head?

- What feelings might this man be experiencing?

- What beliefs does this man have, or what assumptions is this man making?

If you really want to challenge the child, you can also think about the thoughts that might be in the dog's head.

As we have seen, there are many skills involved in the development of ToM. In order to attempt to understand someone else's perspective, feelings, thoughts, beliefs, or assumptions, we must be able to read their nonverbal signals, understand emotions in others and ourselves, and use flexible thinking.

Interventions

Given the above-mentioned interaction between ToM and relationship skills, a few intervention strategies for relationship skills are described below. Challenges with social interactions can negatively impact emotion regulation. The following are sample activities that might strengthen relationship skills.

Appendix

Decoding

Watch a television show with the child or adolescent that has people or other expressive characters in it, look at pictures of peoples' faces in magazines, or watch video clips of people. Work together to assess and discuss the following:

- What feeling is the person having? You can look for both positive and negative feelings.

- What clues can you identify in their body language that they are feeling this way? You might want to encourage the child to look at their eyes, eyebrows, evidence of wrinkles on their forehead or around the eyes, the shape of the mouth, the way their cheeks curve, the position of their arms, and whether or not their face looks flushed, pale, or how you might typically expect.

- How do you think their body is feeling as a result of these feelings? Where do you think they are feeling the emotions?

- What might have caused the person to feel that way? If you are watching a television show with the child and have the ability to rewind, it might be helpful to watch a scene once and then rewind to look for further clues. If you are reading a book, read the scene again for clues. If you are looking in a magazine, look at the contextual clues in the picture. (*Contextual clues* are the things that are happening in the background.) For example, perhaps the character in the show has a favorite chair at the dinner table and someone else sat in her favorite chair. You can assist the child with looking for this important contextual information as you assess the expression of feeling on the character's face and discuss the way the person's body might feel. On the other hand, perhaps the character put on a swimsuit to run through the sprinkler and a quick camera shot of the window shows rain. Your child might then be able to anticipate the way the character feels based on background and contextual clues.

- Based upon the child's observations, how would she rate the intensity of the feelings the person is having? Small? Medium? Big?

EMOTION REGULATION

- What strategies might the person in the video, picture, or show use to decrease the intensity of the feeling they are having (if the feeling the child observed was negative)?

Decoding Part II

Talk with the child to decide whether the first activity helped them decode feelings more accurately. Is the child noticing things about body language that they did not before? Can they identify feelings more quickly? Are they able to examine contextual clues for more information? Are they able to identify the body parts in which they feel feelings? Talk with the child about honing their social detective skills or ability to observe different components of social interactions. These observations will help them look for social cues and clues in their everyday interactions. The child can subtly observe others. (Teach the meaning of *subtly* by demonstrating the difference between glancing and staring.) Recognizing the subtle (and not so subtle) nuances of social interaction will help the child increase their social skills, social reactions, and social problem-solving, which will, in turn, help them increase their ability to regulate emotionally.

Decoding Part III

You can also complete the above exercise with picture books or graphic novels. If you are working with a young child, they will love this exercise. If you are working with an older child or adolescent, you can ask them to help you decode emotions for another child with whom you are spending time. Children and adolescents enjoy helping others. A sample list of picture books can be found in the Resources section.

Action List

Work with the child to create a collage, list, journal, or note cards that list strategies that have helped them in the past when they have experienced intensely negative feelings in a social situation. For example:

- **Situation:** The child saw a picture on Instagram that included many of her friends. It looked like they were at a party in which she was not included.

- **Feeling:** Hurt, disappointed, embarrassed, angry.

Appendix

- **Strategy:** Instead of writing a nasty comment on Instagram, letting her feelings overwhelm her, or saying something mean to one of her friends, the child talked herself through it. She reminded herself that she is not very close with the person who hosted the party and that she probably wouldn't invite her to a party either. She told herself that it was okay to feel disappointed, and then she distracted herself with her favorite book.

The Tricky Balance in a Conversation

In order to ensure reciprocity (the back-and-forth in a conversation) and shared enjoyment (mutual enjoyment) in a social interaction, it is generally important to be sure that we are listening as much as, if not *more* than, we are talking. Listening is a critical part of social interaction. The next time the child spends time with someone, encourage them to make sure they are listening a lot. Explain the difference between listening to understand versus listening to respond. The more success the child feels in social interactions, the less anxiety they might experience, and the more they will be able to manage their feelings. For more information and strategies, please see *Talk with Me* (Mataya et al. 2017).

Flexible Thinking

Flexible thinking contributes to our ability to regulate our emotions effectively. Many of the activities throughout this book offer strategies that might help the child or adolescent cope with changes in schedules, routines, and expectations. Know the child. If minor changes still cause the child to become dysregulated, proceed with caution with the following flexible thinking strategies. You might want to begin with very small, manageable, relatively unimportant changes before proceeding to higher flexible thinking demands. Here are flexible thinking activities you might try:

- If the child sits in a particular seat in a classroom, encourage them to ask their teacher for permission to switch seats one day. (If the teacher does not require permission, the child can just switch seats.)

- If the child sits at a particular seat at the dinner, lunch, or breakfast table at home, switch places one day.

- Encourage the child to eat breakfast for dinner and dinner for breakfast.

EMOTION REGULATION

- Suggest the child walk a different way to class than they typically do.

- Perhaps the child can walk a different way home from school than they typically do.

- Have the child imagine they are using a Silly Putty brain in situations in which they tend to be more rigid. Explain there are two types of brains—a rock brain or our lizard brain (anxious/rigid brain) or a Silly Putty or wizard brain (problem-solving brain) (Barry 2006). Silly Putty brains are more fun than rock brains. Silly Putty bends, stretches, and can be molded into cool creations.

- If the child drinks the same drink for lunch, encourage them to switch it.

- If the child likes a particular brand of chips, encourage them to try a new brand.

- Explain the concept of a brain-poline (brain trampoline) to the child. Our brain-polines give us the ability to flex our brains. Your child can jump from black-and-white thinking ("I'm going to eat a taco for lunch or I'm not eating at all) to the rainbow in between (Since we're out of taco shells, I'll eat a sandwich instead) (Kerstein 2013).

For more ideas, see Kerstein (2013).

This Appendix offered a handful of strategies for increasing the child's skills in the areas of interoception, motor skills, ToM, and flexible thinking. These strategies will hopefully help the child as they continue their journey to more effective emotion regulation.

APPENDIX

EXERCISES AND ACTIVITIES TO SUPPORT EMOTION REGULATION

Table 1: GOALS

Name: _____   Date: _____

Professional   Child/Adolescent   Caregiver

EMOTION REGULATION

Table 2.1: MY EMOTION REGULATION

Name: _____   Date: _____

Directions: Answer the following questions using a 4-point scale.
1 = strongly disagree;   2 = agree;   3 = disagree;   4 = strongly disagree.

1. When I want to feel more *positive* emotions (such as joy or amusement), I change what I'm thinking about.   1   2   3   4

2. I keep my emotions to myself.   1   2   3   4

3. When I want to feel fewer *negative* emotions (such as sadness or anger), I change what I'm thinking about.   1   2   3   4

4. I am a person who takes control of my emotions by managing my thoughts and reactions.   1   2   3   4

5. I let my feelings drive my thoughts and reactions.   1   2   3   4

Appendix

Table 2.2: STRENGTHS

Name: _____   Date: _____

__ The ability to notice small details and pieces of information

__ The ability to look at the big picture in a situation

__ The ability to think deeply about a topic

__ The ability to be organized

__ The capacity for empathy

__ The ability to be kind

__ A talent in logical reasoning

__ An interest in morality and rules

__ The ability to memorize information quickly

__ A large vocabulary

__ A lot of knowledge about particular subjects

__ An inquisitive nature

__ A good memory

__ A sense of humor

__ The ability to pick up on new information quickly

__ The ability to form close relationships

__ The desire to help others

__ The desire to please others

__ Other (please complete)

__ Other (please complete)

EMOTION REGULATION

Table 2.3: STUDENT STRENGTHS

Name: _____ Date: _____

The child or adolescent has the following strengths: This child or adolescent is also good at:

1.

2.

3.

4.

5.

6.

7.

8.

9.

10.

Again, as you work with the child, it will not only be helpful to share the strengths you have identified, but also important to ask the child to reflect upon the strengths they see in themselves.

Table 3.1: POSSIBLE CHARACTERISTICS OF DEPRESSION

Name: _____ Date: _____

- Complaints of feeling sick
- School refusal
- Refusal to attend social functions
- Increased neediness or clinginess
- Extreme worry about such issues as a parent dying or things going wrong
- Increased trouble at school
- Feelings of irritability
- Feelings of isolation
- An increase in sleeping or a change in eating patterns
- Increased crying
- Disinterest in activities that were previously enjoyed (Briers 2009; Chansky 2008)

Appendix

Figure 4.1: Pause! Notice Your Surroundings

Name: _____   Date: _____

Take a moment to notice the details around you. Don't analyze them, judge them, or formulate a response of any sort. Just notice! What do you see? Hear? Smell? Taste? What are you touching? Where are you? How does your body feel? What emotions are you experiencing?

Take a moment to write them down or talk through them:

EMOTION REGULATION

Table 4.1: NEGATIVE TRIGGERS

Name: _____   Date: _____

Directions: Circle the number that describes the degree of intensity of the trigger in each situation.
1 = small trigger;   2 = medium trigger;   3 = big trigger

Being invited to a party	1	2	3
Hearing a loud noise	1	2	3
Someone not believing you	1	2	3
Your friend not being able to hang out	1	2	3
The smell of certain foods	1	2	3
A new challenge	1	2	3
Being left out when other people are together	1	2	3
Doing poorly on a test	1	2	3
Someone yelling (not necessarily at you)	1	2	3
Missing your favorite show	1	2	3
Being out of your favorite food	1	2	3
Bright lights	1	2	3
Having a cold	1	2	3
Feeling out of control because someone else is being bossy	1	2	3
Making a mistake	1	2	3
Feeling unsure what to do because you're in a new place	1	2	3
People being mean to you	1	2	3
Getting hurt	1	2	3
Needing food because you're hungry	1	2	3
Not getting enough sleep	1	2	3
Something bad happening	1	2	3
Your birthday	1	2	3
Being told to put away something you don't want to	1	2	3

Appendix

Table 4.2: POSITIVE TRIGGERS

Name: _____   Date: _____

Directions: Circle the number that describes the degree of intensity of the trigger in each situation.
1 = small trigger;   2 = medium trigger;   3 = big trigger

Situation	Small	Medium	Big
Being invited to a party	1	2	3
Spending time with a friend	1	2	3
Seeing your mom	1	2	3
Seeing your dad	1	2	3
Your birthday	1	2	3
Drinking your favorite drink	1	2	3
Eating your favorite food	1	2	3
Being at the beach	1	2	3
Reading a good book	1	2	3
Listening to music	1	2	3
People being treated fairly	1	2	3
Someone being kind to you	1	2	3
Feeling healthy	1	2	3
Dancing	1	2	3
Singing	1	2	3
A sunny day	1	2	3
Gaming	1	2	3
Watching a movie	1	2	3
Having extra time to spend with your hobbies or interests	1	2	3

EMOTION REGULATION

Table 4.3: TRICKY TRIGGERS

Name: _____   Date: _____

Triggers	This Is Harder When ...	This Would Not Bother Me as Much When ...
Hearing a loud noise		
Someone not believing you		
Your friend not being able to hang out		
The smell of certain foods		
A new challenge		
Being left out when other people are together		
Doing poorly on a test		
Someone yelling (not necessarily at you)		
Missing your favorite show		
Being out of your favorite food		
Bright lights		
Having a cold		
Feeling out of control because someone is being bossy		
Making a mistake		
Being unsure of what to do because you are in a new place		
People being mean to you		

Appendix

Getting hurt

Needing food because you're hungry

Not getting enough sleep

Something bad happening

Your birthday

Being invited to a party

Spending time with a friend

Seeing your mom

Seeing your dad

Drinking your favorite drink

Eating your favorite food

Being at the beach

Reading a good book

People being treated fairly

Someone being kind to you

Feeling healthy

Dancing

Singing

A sunny day

Gaming

Watching a movie

EMOTION REGULATION

Figure 4.5: Triggered responses

Name: _____ Date: _____

Appendix

Figure 4.6: Positive Experience Plan

Name: _____   Date: _____

I plan to add the following experiences to my life in order to increase my positive feelings. (These experiences could be swinging on a swing, a trip to the library, riding a bike, taking a walk, reading a favorite book, drawing, or anything that helps the child feel more positive.):

1. _____

2. _____

3. _____

4. _____

5. _____

Figure 4.7: X-Ray Machine

Name: _____   Date: _____

Ask the child: If the mirror was like an x-ray machine and you could look inside yourself, what would you see? What beliefs do you have about yourself? The following are examples of possible core beliefs the child may have. The examples show both positive and negative core beliefs.

1. I am: _____

2. I can: _____

3. I always: _____

4. I wish I: _____

5. People think I'm: _____

EMOTION REGULATION

Figure 4.8: Look in the Mirror

Name: _____   Date: _____

You can also work with the child to identify core beliefs through the following activity.

When you look in the mirror, what do you see? I see: _____

How much do you like what you see?   0   1   2   3   4   5

When you look in the mirror, what do you see? I see: _____

How much do you like what you see?   0   1   2   3   4   5

When you look in the mirror, what do you see? I see: _____

How much do you like what you see?   0   1   2   3   4   5

When you look in the mirror, what do you see? I see: _____

How much do you like what you see?   0   1   2   3   4   5

When you look in the mirror, what do you see? I see: _____

How much do you like what you see?   0   1   2   3   4   5

Appendix

Table 4.4: ORIGIN OF CORE BELIEFS

Name: _____   Date: _____

Core belief	I think this started when …

Table 4.5: CORE BELIEFS AND ASSUMPTIONS

Name: _____   Date: _____

Core belief	Assumption

EMOTION REGULATION

Table 4.6: IMPACT OF CORE BELIEFS

Name: _____   Date: _____

Core belief	Assumption	Things I do/don't do because of core belief

Table 4.7: FIND MY STRENGTHS TO CHALLENGE ASSUMPTIONS

Name: _____   Date: _____

Core belief	Assumption	Challenging the assumption and finding my strengths

Appendix

Table 4.8: NEW CORE BELIEFS

Name: _____   Date: _____

Core belief	New core belief

EMOTION REGULATION

Figure 4.13: Flip It

Name: _____   Date: _____

Appendix

Table 4.9: SHRINK THE LIZARD THOUGHTS

Name: _____   Date: _____

Distorted Thought	This Is a Reasonable Thought Because ...	This New Thought Will Help Me Manage My Emotions

EMOTION REGULATION

Table 4.10: EVALUATE YOUR THINKING

Name: _____   Date: _____

Positive Thought	This Thought Was Triggered By ...	These Positive Thoughts Helped Me Feel ...	Take Action

Appendix

Table 4.11: EMOTION INTENSITY

Feeling	Intensity	Situations	Strategies
Angry	HIGH		
	MEDIUM		
	LOW		
Sad	HIGH		
	MEDIUM		
	LOW		
Nervous	HIGH		
	MEDIUM		
	LOW		

EMOTION REGULATION

Note: The concept of using shading to illustrate the intensity of feelings in this model is adapted from Jaffe and Gardner, *My Book Full of Feelings: How to Control and React to the Size of Your Emotions* (2006).

Feeling	Intensity	Situations	Strategies
Scared	HIGH		
	MEDIUM		
	LOW		
Happy	HIGH		
	MEDIUM		
	LOW		
Calm	HIGH		
	MEDIUM		
	LOW		

Appendix

Table 4.12: EMOTIONAL STRENGTH

Name: _____   Date: _____

Things That Increase My Emotional Strength	Things That Make Me Vulnerable to Emotional Meltdowns

EMOTION REGULATION

Figure 4.23: Think like a wizard.

Name: _____ Date: _____

Appendix

Figure 5.1: What Have You Learned?

Name: _____   Date: _____

What have you learned about yourself while reading this book?

What do you plan to do with this knowledge?

What activities help you manage your emotions better?

What situations make it harder for you to manage your emotions?

EMOTION REGULATION

Figure 5.2: My Toolbox

Name: _____ Date: _____

THE WAY I SEE IT

Series by Dr. Temple Grandin

FUTURE HORIZONS   www.fhautism.com | 817•277•0727

Did you like this book?

Rate it and share your opinion!

BARNES & NOBLE
BOOKSELLERS
www.bn.com

amazon.com

Not what you expected? Tell us!

Most negative reviews occur when the book did not reach expectation. Did the description build any expectations that were not met? Let us know how we can do better.

Please drop us a line at info@fhautism.com.
Thank you so much for your support!

FUTURE   HORIZONS

www.ingramcontent.com/pod-product-compliance
Lightning Source LLC
Jackson TN
JSHW061942020725
86889JS00002B/2